THE GILL HISTORY OF IRELAND

General Editors: JAMES LYDON, PH.D.
MARGARET MACCURTAIN, PH.D.

D0023934

Other titles in the series

THE
MODERNISATION
OF
IRISH SOCIETY
1848-1918

Joseph Lee

GILL AND MACMILLAN

Published by
Gill and Macmillan Ltd.
2 Belvedere Place
Dublin 1
and in association with the
Macmillan
Group of Publishing Companies

Cover design by Cor Klaasen
Illustration: Michael Boyton burning leases of the Duke of Leinster on a
'98 pike' (Illustrated London News 1880)

7171 0567 9

Produced in Ireland at The Richview Press Limited.

Contents

Foreword

THE study of Irish history has changed greatly in recent decades, as more evidence becomes available and new insights are provided by the growing number of historians. It is natural, too, that with each generation new questions should be asked about our past. The time has come for a new large-scale history. It is the aim of the Gill History of Ireland to provide this. This series of studies of Irish history, each written by a specialist, is arranged chronologically. But each volume is intended to stand on its own and no attempt has been made to present a uniform history. Diversity of analysis and interpretation is the aim; a group of young historians have tried to express the view of their generation on our past. It is the hope of the editors that the series will help the reader to appreciate in a new way the rich heritage of Ireland's history.

JAMES LYDON, PH.D.
MARGARET MACCURTAIN, PH.D.

Do mo mháthair agus i
ndíl-chuimhne m'athar.

Preface

THIS study was originally conceived more as a work of reflection than of research. Unfortunately, despite many splendid recent contributions to the history of the high politics of the period, the present state of knowledge precludes an interpretative essay of the type envisaged. Scholars regularly and rightly lament the neglect of Irish economic history. Several other fields lie equally fallow, scarcely sprouting even a crop of weeds. Intellectual history, the ultimate key to our understanding of both economy and society, has hardly impinged on scholarly consciousness. The history of education has been treated virtually exclusively as a mere branch of the diplomatic history of church-state relations. Voting patterns have been widely ignored; not a single general election has been studied in adequate local detail. The present essay cannot, needless to say, fill these gaps. It burrows tentatively in a few unfamiliar directions, but neither time nor space permit more than a prolegomenon to a sustained study of the modernisation process in Ireland.

Despite the revised concept of the work, I have, perhaps rashly, retained the original title in the hope that, as a term widely, if ambiguously, used in international scholarship, modernisation may prove immune to the parochial preoccupations implicit in equally elusive and more emotive concepts like gaelicisation and anglicisation. Modernisation is defined as the growth of equality of opportunity. This requires that merit supersede birth as the main criterion for the distribution of income, status and power, and this, in turn, involves the creation of political consciousness among the masses, the decline of deference based on inherited status, and the growth of functional specialisation, without which merit can hardly begin to be measured.

It is a vulgar error to confuse terminology with thought. New terminology may merely mean glossier, and perhaps shoddier, packaging of familiar products. I hope, therefore, particularly as references are confined to original sources, that the bibliography indicates my heavy obligation to other scholars. More specifically, I have accumulated immense debts to Margaret MacCurtain, who has indulged the idiosyncracies of a wayward contributor with true Dominican resignation to the inscrutable designs of providence. Paul Bew, Gearóid Ó Tuathaigh, E. D. Steele and John Vincent have not only set several trains of thought in motion but brought many others grinding to a timely halt. They must not, of course, be held responsible for derailments due to drunken driving. My wife, Anne, has been a constant support, whether in typing at short notice into the small hours or rescuing me from the infuriating clutches of uninvited guests!

I am grateful to the Master and Fellows of Peterhouse for sustaining an atmosphere conducive to amiable reflection on the nature of Irish identity.

Joseph Lee

Peterhouse,
Cambridge.

1 Economy and Society

Population

A t least 800,000 people, about 10 per cent of the population, died from hunger and disease between 1845 and 1851. But there was nothing unique, by the standards of pre-industrial subsistence crises, about the famine. The death rate had been frequently equalled in earlier European famines, including, possibly, in Ireland itself during 1740–41. Despite death and emigration the population in 1851, 6.6 million, was still among the highest ever recorded. Population had, moreover, usually recovered rapidly from earlier famines. But, far from recovering after 1851, it fell to 4.4 million by 1911. What was peculiar, therefore, was not the famine, but the long-term response of Irish society to this short-term calamity.

Six main factors influenced post-famine demographic development: the changing rural class structure, rising age at marriage, declining marriage and birth rates, a static death rate and emigration. The combination of these six factors was unique to Ireland, but they did not combine within the country in precisely the same manner from decade to decade or from province to province, resulting, as can be seen from the following table, in marked regional fluctuations in the pace of population decline.

Rate of Population Decline (%)

	Leinster	Munster	Ulster	Connacht	Ireland
1841–51	15·3	22·5	15·7	28·8	19·9
1851–61	12·9	18·5	4·8	9·6	11·5
1861–71	8·1	7·9	4·2	7·3	6·7
1871–81	4·5	4·5	4·9	2·9	4·4
1881–91	7·1	11·9	7·1	11·8	9·1
1891–1901	3·3	8·3	2·3	10·1	5·2
1901–11	+0·8	3·8	0·1	5·6	1·5
1841–1911	41·2	56·8	33·8	57·0	46·4

The enumeration of many farmers' children as labourers in the census of 1841 complicates calculation of the precise number of landless labourers, but even a rough estimate shows that the famine initiated a transformation in rural social structure.

	Labourers	Cottiers (under 5 acres)	Farmers (5–15 acres)	(over 15 acres)
1845	700,000	300,000	310,000	277,000
1851	500,000	88,000	192,000	290,000
1910	300,000	62,000	154,000	304,000

Between 1845 and 1851 the number of labourers and cottiers fell 40 per cent, the number of farmers 20 per cent. During the following 60 years the number of labourers and cottiers again fell about 40 per cent, the number of farmers only 5 per cent. Within the rural community the class balance swung sharply in favour of farmers, and within the farming community it swung even more sharply in favour of bigger and against smaller farmers.

These striking shifts in rural social structure may help explain one of the most intractable problems to perplex students of nineteenth-century Ireland, the apparently abrupt reversal of demographic direction involved in converting the Irish from one of the earliest marrying to the latest and most rarely marrying people in Europe. Between 1845 and 1914 average male age at marriage rose from about 25 to 33, average female age from about 21 to 28. The decline in crude marriage rate (the number of marriages per 1,000 of the population) from about 7 in the immediate pre-famine period to about 5 by 1880, and the increase in the proportion of females in the age group 45–54 never married, from 12 per cent in 1851 to 26 per cent in 1911, distinguished Ireland as a demographic freak.

Such striking changes appear to indicate an entirely new mentality among the survivors of the holocaust, to represent a sharp reversal of existing patterns of behaviour. The change has been widely associated with the switch from sub-division of land among all sons to inheritance by only one child. According to this interpretation, land was subordinated to people before the famine: henceforth people were subordinated to land. Sub-division meant inheritance for all sons, young marriages, large families. Consolidation condemned the younger children to the emigrant ship or the shelf. For the inheritor it entailed postponing marriage until the parental farm became available. This interpretation, though partially valid, greatly exaggerates the scale and speed of the transformation. Age at marriage in pre-famine Ireland probably varied more or less directly with the value of the farm. Within any given region, labourers and cottiers married earlier than small farmers, who in turn married earlier than larger farmers. Sub-division was largely confined, for a generation before the famine, to already small farms in the far west. In the rest of the country even small farmers generally insisted on a dowry from the daughter-in-law and rarely subdivided. A disproportionate number of famine survivors belonged to classes with above average age at marriage, already unaccustomed to sub-divide. Even had age at marriage remained unchanged within social groups, the reduction in the proportion of earlier marrying strata would have raised average age at marriage. The sizes of strata changed more than their behaviour. Age at marriage within groups gradually increased, but the overall change did not require the whole peasantry to revolutionise their attitude under the cathartic impact of the tragedy, but rather required the surviving labourers and cottiers, who previously had little to lose from early marriage, to adopt the existing attitudes of more prudent calculators. However much these attitudes hardened and sharpened in the congenial post-famine circumstances, they were inherited rather than created by post-famine man.

As the rungs on the social ladder widened, as the cottier disappeared and the average size of farm increased, it became increasingly difficult to marry a little above or a little beneath oneself. The range of social choice for bidders in the marriage market narrowed. Mixed marriages, between farmers and labourers, were considered unnatural. Farmers' children preferred celibacy to labourers. The increasing longevity of parents reinforced the drift towards late marriage. In 1841 only 6·3 per cent of the population were over 60, by 1901 eleven per cent. Sons, more patient in waiting for a farm than daughters for a man, became relatively older than their brides. This widening age gap meant that a larger number of wives became, in due course, widows. Wives and widows, victims of largely loveless matches, projected their frustrated capacity for affection onto their sons, and contemplated with dread the prospect of a 'rival' daughter-in-law who might supplant them in their sons' affections. The farmers' wives gave a grimly ironic twist to Parnell's famous warning 'keep a firm grip on your homesteads'. To farming mothers the daughter-in-law posed a more pernicious threat than the landlord, and many a mother devoted her later life sapping her son's will to relegate her to the end room in favour of another woman. As a result the proportion of female farmers, frequently widows refusing to make over the farm to a son, rose from four to fifteen per cent between 1841 and 1911.

The Churches, particularly the Catholic Church, are frequently criticised for contributing to the unnatural marriage patterns in post-famine Ireland by treating sex as a satanic snare and exalting the virtues of celibacy. The Churches however, merely reflected the dominant economic values of post-famine rural society. 'The average Irish peasant' it was observed, 'takes unto himself a mate with as clear a head, as placid a heart and as steady a nerve as if he were buying a cow at Ballinasloe Fair'. Few societies anywhere, rural or urban, Christian or Confucian, refined the marriage bargain to such an acquisitive nicety. The integrity of the family was ruthlessly sacrificed, generation after generation, to the priority of economic man, to the rationale of the economic calculus. Priests and parsons, products and prisoners of the same society, dutifully sanctified this mercenary ethos, but they were in any case powerless to challenge the primacy of economic man over the Irish countryside.

Clergymen played useful roles as psychological safety valves by helping to reconcile the celibate to their condition. Protestant illegitimacy rates, though slightly higher than Catholic, were distinctly lower than in the rest of the United Kingdom, or, indeed, than in most continental Catholic communities. In the comparative context, the similarities between the sexual and marital mores of Irish Catholics and Protestants were far more striking than the local differences on which polemicists loved to linger. It seems probable that only the consolation offered by the Churches to the celibate victims of economic man prevented lunacy rates, which quadrupled between 1850 and 1914, from rising even more rapidly.

Increasingly late and rare marriage resulted in a fall in crude birthrate (the number of births per 1,000 of the population) from over 35 before the famine to 28 by 1870 and 23 by 1914. Most European societies reduced their birth rate in the late nineteenth century, generally through limiting the size rather than the number of families. In other countries, however, falling death rates helped offset the decline in birth rate. Ironically, this process occurred much more slowly in Ireland, which had one of the lowest normal death rates in Europe, due mainly to a remarkably low infant mortality rate. The pervasive breast feeding of babies, and the nutritious potato diet kept the proportion of deaths among infants in their first year below ten per cent, compared with about twenty per cent in most European countries. The graphs illustrate the exceptional nature of Irish birth and death rates.

A death rate of 17 subtracted from a birth rate of 23, the usual situation between 1890 and 1914, should result in a population increase of 6 per 1,000. Emigration, however, siphoned off more than this natural increase. Close on 2,000,000 emigrants fled between 1848 and 1855; another 3,500,000 followed by 1914. Until 1851

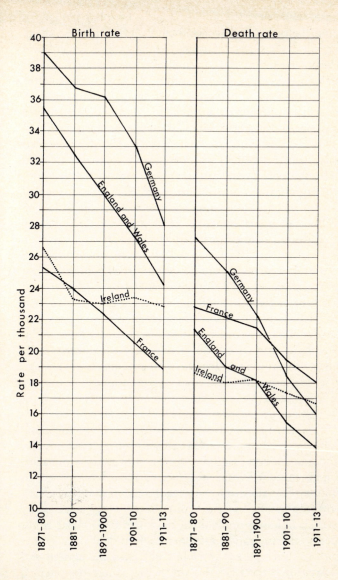

Birth rate

Death rate

Rate per thousand

Germany

England and Wales

Ireland

France

Germany

France

England and Wales

Ireland

1871–80 1881–90 1891–1900 1901–10 1911–13 1871–80 1881–90 1891–1900 1901–10 1911–13

the exodus consisted predominantly of small farmers in family groups. As the number of agricultural holdings stabilised after 1851, farmers' children and agricultural labourers leaving as individuals replaced family groups as the main source of emigration. The flow declined after the mid-1850s, fluctuating according to the relative prosperity of America and Ireland. Numbers rose to over 100,000 in 1863 and 1864 following bad harvests, fell as low as 30,000 in 1877, when American slump coincided with Irish prosperity, and rose steeply to 96,000 in 1880 when American recovery coincided with Irish depression.

Emigration among labourers reflected more a revolution in their subjective mentalities than in the objective realities of their standard of living. Average weekly agricultural wages rose from 5/- in 1845 to 7/- in 1870 and 11/- in 1914. The crux of the matter was that the rise in the labourer's standard of living lagged behind the rise in his aspirations. The agricultural labourer who told an enquirer in 1894 'I don't like the work on the land. It is very laborious and does not lead to anything. I have seen men who have worked all their lives as badly off as at the beginning' expressed the sentiments of thousands of emigrants no longer satisfied with a traditional existence. That the emigration of small farmers was also as much a psychological as an economic phenomenon, that it constituted an aspect of the modernisation of Irish mentalities, can be seen from the persistence into the post-famine period of pre-famine patterns of regional population movements. Emigration was lowest in Connacht, where the survivors, still too poor and backward to contemplate alternatives to traditional existence, lacking both the means and the will to leave, clung tenaciously to their holdings or eked out new ones from waste lands. Connacht emigration rates gradually caught up with the national average by 1870, but not until the agricultural depression after 1877 did the heavy emigration, which has since characterised the province, begin. Between 1871 and 1881 the population of Connacht fell only three per cent, two-thirds the national average, whereas between 1881 and 1891 it fell twelve per cent, one and a half times the national average.

Economic change

The flight from the land became widespread throughout western Europe in the late nineteenth century. Irish experience was peculiar mainly because it involved higher emigration, and lower internal migration, than the European average, and because it was the only European country whose rural population actually fell. Why did Ireland, outside the Lagan Valley, fail to create her own Bostons and Birminghams? Why did the population of Belfast increase from 100,000 to 400,000 between 1850 and 1914, while that of Dublin only managed to creep up from 250,000 to 300,000?

The root of the problem in many backward economies lies in agriculture. Food supply constitutes a serious bottleneck because productivity is so low that a sufficient surplus to feed a substantial non-agricultural population cannot be generated. This was not the case in Ireland, which remained a substantial net exporter of food throughout the period. Nevertheless, agriculture made nothing like its potential contribution to economic growth. This failure has been traditionally explained in terms of the switch from tillage to pasture after the famine as 'the landlord and the bullock drove the people off the land'. The debate on the relative merits of livestock and tillage tends to obscure the fact that both sectors contributed to considerable agricultural progress between 1750 and 1860. Rotation, revolving primarily around the potato, stimulated increases in corn and root yields, which generally compared well with European averages. Density of stocking increased sharply between

1840 and 1860, but it stagnated subsequently. Commercial farming had superseded subsistence agriculture over three-quarters of the country by 1850, when Ireland had one of the most commercially advanced agricultures in the world.

After the famine farmers responded promptly to price movements, which generally favoured livestock more than grain. Profit margins in the livestock sector benefited not only from rapidly rising prices, but also from the fact that production costs rose more slowly in labour-extensive pasture than in labour-intensive tillage. Cattle numbers doubled from 2·7 million in 1848 to 5 million in 1914: sheep numbers, fluctuating violently, rose from 2 million in 1848 to 3·6 million in 1914: poultry numbers, though temporarily decimated in the famine, rose from less than 10 million in 1841 to 27 million in 1914. In 1845 potatoes, grain and livestock each accounted for about one-third of the value of agricultural output. By 1914 the livestock sector contributed three-quarters of the total value. Climate and soil, in contrast to continental experience, allowed the farmer to move exceptionally easily between tillage and livestock and although his gross income from pasture was lower than had he concentrated on tillage, his net income – his prime consideration – fell only slightly below what he could have achieved through a great deal extra effort. The Irish farmer behaved as a rational economic man, and, after the wave of famine evictions ebbed, it was he, not the landlord, who drove his children and the labourers off the land. But while the farmer behaved rationally within his terms of economic reference, those terms frequently proved dangerously restrictive. As the age of inheritance and the proportion of widows gradually increased, the likelihood of the 'young' generation proving receptive to technical progress diminished. The range of efficiency among farmers appears to have been exceptionally wide, and even within the livestock sector the difference between the actual and potential output – had all farmers reached the existing 'best practice' standards – seems to have been substantial. The farmer showed more commercial than technical alertness, and it remains unclear to what extent his high leisure preference reflected conscious choice. The propensity for livestock production reduced both the potential rural demand for labour and the potential size of the agricultural market for goods and services; the propensity for inefficient livestock production reduced them still further. A combination of climate and soil on the one hand, and the peculiar family structure on the other, made the potential divergence between individual and collective rationality exceptionally wide in Irish agriculture.

Labour supply posed as few problems as food supply. The supply of unskilled labour obviously exceeded demand, and the supply of skilled labour responded quickly to demand. Scottish and English workers were imported into Belfast to instruct the locals in the mysteries of the machine age, but the natives proved apt apprentices. There is little reason to doubt that the same would have been the case had businessmen attempted to establish major industrial enterprises in other areas. In some sectors, indeed, cheap labour, as James Connolly rightly argued, deprived employers of the stimulus of rising labour costs to increase efficiency.

Recent research has not substantiated the once fashionable belief that lack of capital frustrated industrialisation. In comparison with the requirements for even large scale manufacturing enterprises, ample amounts of capital were invested in government bonds and municipal loans, or left on sterile deposit in banks. Bank deposits rose from £16 million in 1859 to £33 million in 1877, then stagnated until 1890, before rising to £60 million by 1913. Deposits provide, however, a deceptive index of savings. The increase in the number of branches from 170 in 1845 to 569 in 1880 allowed banks to tap hitherto hoarded savings. Some of the increase in deposits before 1880 simply reflected a transfer of savings from the mattress to the bank safe. Although the average standard of living increased sharply between 1848 and 1877, the actual standard of living rose only slowly. The increase in *per capita* incomes reflects the artificial impact of the disappearance of the poorest quarter of the population, whose presence had depressed pre-famine averages, without resulting in a remotely comparable increase in the income of the survivors. Bank branches continued to increase to 809 in 1910, but the doubling of deposits in the twenty years before the First World War represents a genuine increase in savings, as new branches were by this stage established mainly in existing banking centres. The alacrity with which Irish purchasers, urban and rural, bought encumbered estates in the 1850s to the value of £20,000,000 pointed to the substantial reservoir of capital seeking outlets in landed property. Capital flowed into railways, gas companies, insurance and shipping firms, and bank shares; but usually only after English investors had borne a disproportionate share of the initial risks and demonstrated to their timid Irish brethren that investment opportunities did actually exist. If Irish industry suffered from a shortage of capital, this was due to the type, not to the amount, of capital available in the country.

Had there been an objective lack of capital the £3–4 million annually abstracted by the Churches, might have deprived the economy of essential capital. However, little potential risk capital found its way into clerical coffers. The clergy probably performed a minor economic service by mobilising otherwise totally unproductive capital and providing some ephemeral employment for local builders.

Shortage of coal and iron precluded imitation of the

English pattern of industrialisation, but not industrialisation itself. Population fell, but its increased purchasing power and growing consumer consciousness actually led to an expansion in the size of the market. The railway integrated the west into the market economy, for though few had been unaffected by, or unfamiliar with, market values in 1845, much of the west lacked sustained exposure, primarily due to prohibitive transport costs, to market influences. Ireland, one of the first European countries to rail-roadise, had 65 miles of track in 1845, 1,000 in 1857, 2,000 in 1872 and, with 3,500 by 1914 boasted one of the densest networks in the world. The railway permitted far greater diffusion of information through the tele-post and the rapid distribution of newspapers. It increased the range of small, personal wants by distributing imports and Dublin goods throughout the countryside, breaking down the stifling barriers of physical and mental self-sufficiency. Between 1861 and 1911 the number of commercial travellers, superseding local pedlars, rose from 500 to 4,500.

Ireland was already a remarkably literate society by 1841, when forty-seven per cent of the population aged over five claimed to be able to read. This proportion rose to fifty-three per cent in 1851 and eighty-eight per cent in 1911. Real literacy fell below these rates, for people exaggerated their reading ability. Nevertheless, the spread of literacy allowed more people to understand advertisements and mail order catalogues, use the parcel post, shop more ambitiously, and generally become more receptive to new consumption patterns. The number of newspapers and periodicals rose from 109 in 1853 to 230 in 1913. The post office distributed twenty million letters in 1914, compared with five million in 1851, a seven-fold *per capita* increase. Ireland was already predominantly English-speaking on the eve of the famine, but the complete triumph of English in the post-famine decades helped spread familiarity with market conventions.

The five-fold increase in imports, from about £15 million to £75 million between 1850 and 1914 reflects the growing market orientation of the Irish consumer. Some of the imports, like tea and coal, could not have been supplied domestically, but there was no apparent reason why a substantial proportion of clothing and footwear imports, which amounted to £12 million per annum by 1914, and a host of miscellaneous consumer goods, ranging from stationery to furniture, could not have been supplied by domestic producers. Virtually the only major expanding market dominated by Irish businessmen was drink. The number of public houses increased from 15,000 in 1850 to nearly 20,000 by 1911, when about £15 million per annum was spent on liquor. Consumption, contrary to Irish reputation, fell slightly below *per capita* English levels. As is customary in gradually urbanising societies – thirty-five per cent of the population lived in towns in 1914 compared with fifteen per cent in 1841 – beer gained at the expense of whiskey. Beer consumption *per capita* increased four-fold, from 40 to 160 pints per annum, while whiskey and poteen consumption probably fell about fifty per cent.

If adequate supplies of food, labour and capital existed, if the size of the market was increasing, to what then can the responsibility for the disappointing rate of economic growth be attributed? Both the success of Belfast, and the failure of Dublin, suggest that considerable importance must be attached to the quality of businessmen. It has become increasingly fashionable among economic historians to denigrate the importance of the entrepreneur, on the grounds that opportunities create businessmen rather than vice versa. The growth of Belfast exposes the inadequacy of this argument. As the expansion of the linen industry slackened after the end of the American

Civil War in 1865, when cotton recaptured many of the markets it had lost to linen during the war, Belfast's prosperity came to rely increasingly on shipbuilding, which grew from virtually nothing in 1850 to pay £20,000 in weekly wages to 12,000 men by 1914. And yet the success of Belfast shipbuilding was largely accidental. Edward Harland came to Belfast in 1854 to become foreman in Robert Hickson's recently established shipbuilding firm, and was on the point of leaving in 1858 to establish his own yard on the Mersey when his harassed employer, who had achieved little success, sold out to him for £5,000. Harland transformed Hickson's struggling yard into one of the greatest in the world, through a combination of technical skill, pioneering new designs in iron ships and in engines, and brilliant salesmanship. His successor as chairman, William James Pirrie, whom Harland made a partner in 1874 at the age of twenty-seven, proved an even more effective salesman, who, as Professor Black puts it, 'not only seized opportunities where they occurred, but as often made them by convincing shipowners of the need to add to their fleets'. Only brilliant entrepreneurship permitted Harland and G. W. Wolff, who became partners in 1860, to overcome the problems that plagued Robert Hickson. Their success in turn paved the way for the rise of another large yard, Workman and Clark, established in 1879 by Frank Workman, who served his apprenticeship in Harland and Wolff, and for the Belfast ropeworks, established in 1878 under G. W. Wolff, which soon became the biggest in the U.K. Had Edward Harland not received Hickson's offer before finalising his plans to transfer to the Mersey in 1858, it seems highly unlikely that shipbuilding and its subsidiary industries would ever have grown to dominate the Belfast economy, and later historians would doubtless dismiss Hickson's yard as a brave but futile venture predestined to collapse by 'lack of opportunity' due to the shortage of raw materials and markets.

One articulate school of thought attributed Belfast's impressive performance primarily to the Protestant ethic. But Belfast's progress after 1848 was increasingly due to immigrant businessmen. Had Belfast relied on local entrepreneurial resources, however ardently Protestant, its growth would have been much less striking. If the Protestant ethic contributed significantly to Belfast's success, something very peculiar must have happened after 1918, when Belfast became the most depressed industrial city in the U.K., a fate not self-evidently related to a decline in the intensity of Belfast Protestantism.

It is as difficult to find convincing evidence of a Catholic ethic in Dublin as of a Protestant in Belfast. A Donegal man who reassured an English visitor solicitous about his leaking roof that 'there will be no drips in heaven' may reflect the classic Catholic concept of time, but Dublin businessmen stoically suffered awkward aspects of Catholic doctrine. Church teaching proved no obstacle to rack-renting slum landlords, frequently ostentatious pillars of Catholic piety, to grinding exploitation of workers, to petty swindling of customers, to learning how to

'fumble in a greasy till
and add the halfpence to the pence
and prayer to shivering prayer'.

Irish Catholicism displayed an obsession with the materialistic which might have made less institutionally religious societies squirm with envy. Not other worldly values, but a very intense 'this worldly' concern with social status characterised Catholic society. This was not in the least surprising. Their social betters, the Protestant upper-classes, preached and practised the social primacy of the professions, particularly of the Church, law and medicine, over trade. As businessmen and their wives sidled their way up the social ladder they realised that the topmost rungs could be reached only by abandoning business – unless they were extraordinarily successful – and acquiring the veneer of gentility. The proportion of Catholic lawyers and doctors rose from about one-third to about one-half between 1861 and 1911. The professional ethic contributed more than the Catholic ethic to the failure of business dynasties to emerge.

There was nothing unusual, in international terms, in the tendency to move out of business as soon as means became available to acquire status in more socially respected occupations. Some observers, it is true, did think the proclivity particularly pronounced in Ireland, and even Benjamin Lee Guinness felt it necessary to guard against the tendency to abandon business by including in his will a provision that if either son should 'unfortunately' retire from the firm, the brewery should go entirely to the other. Even a Guinness could not ignore prevailing fashions. An active extra-business career was not, of course, necessarily incompatible with continuing commercial success. Several of the Guinnesses, Sir Edward Harland and W. J. Pirrie played active roles on the public stage. But they took care not to sacrifice their firms to their other pursuits, to recruit able management and to retain ultimate control.

The temptation to abandon business, or at least to abstract capital from firms to educate children into the professions or, at a more plebian level, into clerkships, was very great. Professional life exercised many attractions, financial as well as cultural. By 1900 lawyers and doctors annual incomes probably averaged close on £1,000, over ten times that of skilled workers' incomes, and probably comparable to the bulk of medium sized business profits. The top professionals expected to earn up to £4,000 per annum. The differential between professional and general incomes was distinctly higher before the First World War than it has since become. Professional careers promised an attractive combination of status, security and comfort. Sensitivity to social considerations was not unique to Ireland. The real problem was that a country relying heavily on its human resources, to compensate for the lack of natural resources, could not afford to indulge this tendency to the same extent as more generously endowed economies.

The lure of the professions exposes the inadequacy of the textbook convention that Ireland had no middle class. Urban Ireland outside Belfast did lack an industrial middle class, but she had, if anything, a surfeit of the professional middle class. The professions accounted for almost as high a proportion of the urban population in Ireland as in England throughout the period, as did domestic servants, familiar status symbols of aspiring middle class gentility.

Doctors and lawyers jostled on the top rungs of the lay status scale, reaping the rewards of the £2–3 million per annum spent on both health and law. Religion cost from £3–4 million per annum, extraordinarily cheap at the price in view of the degree of consumer satisfaction promised by the advertising departments. Between 1851 and 1911 the number of priests increased from 2,500 to 4,000, of monks from 200 to 1,200, of nuns from 1,000 to 9,000, while the number of Protestant clergy, of all denominations, hovered around the 3,000 mark. The number of Catholic clergy, relative both to the size of their own dwindling flock, and to the number of Protestant clergy, increased strikingly. But while priestly productivity fell by half – there was one priest to roughly 1,000 laity in 1911, compared with 2,000 in 1851 – it continued to comfortably exceed that of Protestant clergy, who catered on average to only 500 laity in 1851 and to 400 in 1911. Protestant Ireland was a highly clericalised society and as late as 1914 Protestant soul saving techniques were about twice as labour intensive, and probably three times as capital intensive, as Catholic techniques. The erratic geographical distribution of the Protestant faithful created considerable difficulties in allocating clerical manpower, but the immense social prestige of parson and minister also inflated the supply of clergymen. In addition both Catholic and Anglican communities exported substantial numbers of missionaries. In 1879 the number of Trinity College trained clergymen serving in England was higher than the total number of Church of Ireland clergy in Ireland.

Whatever the reason, few businessmen of international calibre emerged in post-famine Ireland. Other European societies resorted to three main substitutes for inadequate domestic business talent – imported businessmen, investment banks and the government. Immigrant businessmen did, in fact, make a major contribution to Irish economic development. Belfast owed much of its growth to them. The shipbuilding industry was originally established in Belfast in 1791 by William Ritchie from Ayr. Edward Harland was an Englishman; G. W. Wolff was an English-educated German. George Clark, of Workman and Clark, came from Scotland in 1880. The textile machinery industry was dominated by two Scots – James Combe, who established the Falls Foundry in 1845 and James Mackie, who took over the works of yet another Scot, James Scrimgeour in 1858 – and by two immigrants from Leeds, George Horner, who established the Clonard Foundry in 1859 and Steven Cotton, who established the Brookfield Foundry in 1865.

Investment banks provided a frequent continental solution to the problem of economic retardation. Crudely, the investment banker acted not only as a banker, but as an entrepreneur also, by investing deposits directly in industry. In effect, he took more risks to achieve higher profits. Successful investment banks served as major engines of economic development by allowing exceptionally enterprising individuals to promote firms in several sectors simultaneously. The risks were considerable, for if one venture failed the others might become involved through no fault of their own. Mortality rates among investment banks were high enough to caution prudence, but, on the other hand, when bankers disciplined enthusiasm by discretion they played important roles in industrialisation. The fact that no investment banks emerged in Ireland partly reflects the conservatism of the business community, dominated by the English concept of banking, developed to cater for an economy endowed with an adequate supply of business capacity and therefore unsuited to Irish requirements. But it also reflects the fact that Irish bankers were not hungry fighters. Banking dividends frequently exceeding ten per cent confirm that the commercial sector of the Irish economy subsisted quite comfortably. Unfortunately, in business as in agriculture, private and public interests diverged sharply. The public interest, if defined as the standard of living necessary to persuade potential emigrants to become internal migrants, required an intensive industrialisation drive. The private interest of the commercial sector – importers and exporters, wholesalers, assemblers – the typical cross-section of an enclave economy, simply required to be left in quiet possession of their modest patrimony.

The role of the State

Several continental governments played active roles in reconciling divergencies between private and public welfare. But the fact that England industrialised primarily on the basis of private enterprise decisively influenced English concepts of the proper role of the state in economic development. If the state maintained the sanctity of contracts and the rights of property, it could safely leave individuals to their own enterprise, secure in the conviction that the invisible hand would maximise economic growth. State intervention could only retard the rate of growth.

Crucial consequences followed from this line of reasoning for government attitudes towards Irish economic development. Debate revolved mainly around the theoretical issue of whether, rather than the practical question of how, the state should intervene. England, the workshop of the world, could afford the luxury of intense debate on this question. She had much borrowed time on which to flourish; Ireland had not. Ireland thus became a victim of the peculiarly intense English pre-occupation with the abstract merits of collectivism. The bulk of the Irish people remained utterly indifferent to this bemusing debate, adopting the pragmatic principle of supporting state intervention when it appeared to benefit themselves and opposing it when it did not. A commission of inquiry into the condition of agricultural labourers in 1894 noted among the farmers 'a substratum of annoyance, that such an enquiry should be held, and an opinion that matters between employers and employed chiefly concerned them alone. The labourers, on the other hand, knowing that tenant farmers had benefited by commissions, eagerly welcomed any change which might improve, but could not worsen their conditions' – very human reactions, equally oblivious to the doctrinal niceties of the schools.

This tendency to abstraction in English economic thought, which exerted a debilitating influence on official concepts of the role of the state in economic development, was powerfully reinforced by the role of lawyers in influencing opinion. The majority of 'authoritative' commentators on Irish economic affairs brought a legal training to their task. This predisposed them to subordinate the economic aspects of economic questions to the legal aspects, and to assume that any government measure involving major legal innovations must be of commensurate economic importance. Incantations of the laws of property served as a substitute for thought.

Ireland suffered severely from the consequences of the touching faith of educated opinion in the economic importance of law and in the power of abstract economic theory. This faith absolved its devotees from actually accumulating or analysing information about Irish circumstances. One of the most frequently expressed delusions concerning the formulation of economic policy is that, thanks to over one hundred official inquiries into social and economic aspects of Irish life between 1800 and 1848 'whatever else the government lacked, it was not information'. This is to confuse information with opinions. The numerous inquiries are packed with opinions, based overwhelmingly on local circumstances, virtually useless as guides to policymaking. Little of the regular, systematic information essential to the informed formulation of policy existed for any economic section in 1848 – no data on the size or distribution of national income, no satisfactory information on the factors influencing population change, no detailed statistics on exports and imports, no systematic price indices. More or less reliable agricultural statistics were collected for the first time in 1847, precisely because officials attempting to relieve famine distress found they lacked adequate information on the most elementary facts of rural economic life. Thomas Larcom, probably the best informed English official, took twenty years to realise that Irish farmers thought in terms of Irish instead of English acres! Nothing better illustrates the remoteness from reality of English officialdom than Larcom's prediction in 1850 that the 1851 census would record a population of 7·7 million. It recorded 6·6 million. Larcom, director in chief of famine relief, simply lost a million people in his calculations. Another leading practical 'expert', Professor Longfield, committed himself in 1850 to the immortal prediction that population in 1851 was unlikely to show an increase over that of 1841!

The relative merits of Free Trade and Protection constituted one of the great debates of the century. Few countries in circumstances like Ireland failed to protect their industries to some extent. Yet no comprehensive external trade statistics existed for Ireland between 1825, when records of Anglo-Irish trade ceased to be kept, and 1902, when W. P. Coyne, chief statistician of the newly established department of Agriculture and Technical Instruction, determined to remedy this deficiency. The first returns exposed the inaccuracy of the estimates presented a little earlier by Sir Robert Giffen, the leading English 'authority' on Irish trade.

Even had adequate information generally existed, however, the debate on the land question suggests that little use would have been made of it, so immune were the 'experts' to the virus of evidence. Virtually no analytical reference was made to the voluminous agricultural statistics collected since 1847. One need only compare the contributions of Longfield and de Laveleye, representative of Belgian intellect, to the volume, *Land Tenure in various countries (1870)* to note their contrasting ways of looking at agricultural problems. Longfield, trained – inevitably – as a lawyer, largely ignores the agricultural statistics and concentrates on hypothetical cases concerning the legal niceties of landlord-tenant relations; de Laveleye explores the influence of tenurial forms and size of farm on the volume and structure of agricultural output. Irish and English assessments of the impact of land legislation adopted Longfield's somnambulatory approach. In 1866 J. E. Cairnes concluded that the Encumbered Estates Act of 1849 wrought a revolution in Irish agriculture by replacing 'the weakest and worst of the Irish squirearchy' with men 'whose mercantile instincts will effectually save them from the suicidal rapacity of their predecessors'. John Stuart Mill echoed Cairnes in describing the Act as late as 1871 as 'the greatest boon ever conferred on Ireland by any government'. Neither Cairnes nor Mill, ignoring the agricultural statistics, produced a scrap of serious evidence in support of their assertion. Cairnes' careful investigation into the actual functioning of the Estates Court contrasts strikingly with the casualness of his conclusions concerning the economic impact of the Act. Trained as a lawyer, he simply could not conceive that such mountains of legal labour might bring forth an economic *ridiculus mus*.

In 1864 Professor John Kells Ingram, one of the most luminous Irish intellects of his generation, proposed the introduction of outdoor relief, on the model of the English Poor Law, on the fatuous assumption that this would encourage the Irish small farmer to surrender his holding and become a day labourer, secure in the knowledge that the revised poor law would help him keep body and soul together during his periods of unemployment as a labourer! Ingram devoted intense study to the functioning of the English poor law without it apparently occurring to him to acquaint himself with the attitudes of Irish small farmers. Professor W. L. Burn has argued that one of the causes of delay in land legislation between 1846 and 1870 was simply that no Prime Minister 'had the comprehensive intellectual capacity of Peel or Gladstone. Gladstone's drafting of the Irish Land Bill of 1870, with the assistance of information provided through Chichester Fortescue, was to be one of the most remarkable feats of the century, beyond the powers of Russell, Derby, Aberdeen, Palmerston or Disraeli'. Perhaps. But the information supplied by Chichester Fortescue was quite irrelevant to the issues confronting Irish agriculture, and the Act consequently bore very little relation to Irish reality. Thomas O'Hagan, yet another lawyer congenitally prone to judge the economic influence of a measure according to the importance of the legal principles at issue, president of the Statistical and Social Inquiry Society of Ireland – 'if the Irish Question could only have been put into the hands of a few men like him for quiet settlement . . . how much better would the result have been' mused Goldwin Smith – asserted in 1870 that the value of Gladstone's Land Act 'can scarcely be overestimated'. He adumbrated among 'the vast advantages which no one with the most moderate intelligence can doubt its ability of affording the Irish agriculturist' the decisive inducement to farmers to withdraw their idle hoards from the banks and invest them in the purchase and improvement of land. Nothing of the sort occurred. In this field the 'experts' cannot plead an information gap as an excuse, for only comprehension or credulity gaps can account for their ignoring or misinterpreting the abundant evidence generally available.

Lack of basic information in other areas, therefore, reflected the lack of incisive analysis rather than vice versa. The conviction that they were overtaxed, for instance, united Irishmen of diverse political creeds. Yet the detailed enquiries into the taxation of Ireland in the 1860s and 1890s focussed more on the legal aspects of the taxation clauses of the Act of Union than on the economic implications of the taxation system. The mound of evidence presented contained no thorough enquiry into the impact of taxation on consumption and expenditure patterns. Little wonder, in view of the miserable performance of the 'experts' over the previous half century, that the German, Moritz Bonn, distinguished representative of a different tradition of scholarship, lamented in 1906 the premature death of W. P. Coyne, 'one of the few Irishmen who have brought a scientific training to the treatment of practical questions'.

A certain irony lurks in this *dénouement*. Ingram was one of the pioneers of the historical school in the English-speaking world. Cairnes startled public opinion in 1865 by advocating peasant proprietorship in Ireland. Mill actually enunciated in 1868 the heretical doctrine that 'no one is at all capable of determining what is the right political economy for any country unless he knows its circumstances'. Historians of economic thought rightly emphasise the importance of these contributions to intellectual history, but in practical terms these thinkers did little to develop techniques for discovering a country's 'circumstances'. They remained abstract even in denouncing abstraction.

Similarly, the positive contribution of the state, which has sufficiently impressed some commentators to describe Ireland as England's 'social laboratory', tends to be grossly exaggerated. The state usually intervened in response to short-term disaster – the famine relief works, Arthur Balfour's promotion of light railways and the creation of the Congested Districts Board following the potato failure of 1890 – rather than as part of any long-term, carefully pondered plan. The state devoted no sustained study to any sector of the Irish economy between 1848 and 1914. This approach, ironically, derived support from the fact that the main impetus to intervention came from the engineers, practical men impatient with the lawyers' proclivity for hypothetical musings. The Board of Works, established in 1831, owed its initial momentum to the determination of engineers like Burgoyne, Griffith and Larcom to solve specific problems. But for all their energy and dedication, they were civil, not mechanical engineers, more preoccupied, unless inspired by the transcendent vision of Thomas Drummond, with technical problems of infrastructure – roads, canals, railways, bridges, piers, drainage – than with the economic problems of production. Thus Larcom, under-secretary from 1853 to 1869, had little idea how to extract positive policy recommendations from the statistics on population and agriculture he so diligently compiled.

By English standards, the government did display considerable initiative. But what was daring in the English context appeared timid by continental criteria. The concept of social laboratory implies a degree of experiment and innovation quite unjustified in the wider comparative context. Even in sectors where the state took occasional bold initiatives it then frequently lagged behind developments in England for long periods. Education at the national, secondary and university levels provides a useful example of the nature and limits of state intervention.

The national school system, established in 1831, spread rapidly. The 4,500 schools and 500,000 pupils of 1848 roughly doubled to about 9,000 schools and 1,000,000 pupils in 1914. Originally intended to be undenominational, the system in practice soon became sectarian. Anglicans generally clung to their own schools until the financial retrenchment imposed by disestablishment in 1869 induced them to avail of state subsidy. Catholic and Presbyterian clergy proceeded to establish schools within the system. However, policy played only a relatively minor role in securing the dominance of segrated schools. The simple distribution of population dictated that, in practice, the majority of schools would be denominational. The evidence does not suggest that, where it existed, co-education mellowed animosities imbibed with the mothers' milk. Schools reflected rather than created community sentiments, and proved powerless against the blind hatred lovingly inculcated in the bosom of the Christian family.

The immediate impact of the national schools tends to be exaggerated. In the first two decades they did little more than replace existing educational facilities, not

27

always for the better. They actually reduced the provision made for secondary teaching by displacing teachers who combined instruction at both levels, and the staff student ratio was frequently worse than in existing establishments. The national system, which catered for only twenty-five per cent of the age-group 5–16 during the 1850s, made little contribution to reducing illiteracy before 1860. In 1881, fifty per cent, as late as 1911 thirty-five per cent of pupils attended school less than 100 days a year. The majority of children before 1918 received only 4–5 years schooling, the absolute minimum necessary to cross the threshold level of literacy necessary to undermine traditional attitudes. Contrary to popular persuasion, the schools did not kill the Irish language. Even before the famine the country was predominantly English-speaking. O'Connell spoke in English because most of his east-of-Ireland audiences understood it better than Irish. By 1851 less than ten per cent of the population were unable to speak English, while only thirty per cent were able to speak Irish. The language committed suicide before 1845, aided and abetted less by the national schools than by the hedge schools cherished in nationalist mythology.

Though the language was more a victim of indigenous private enterprise than of state policy, the government certainly intended the national school system to perform a massive brain-washing operation, obliterating subversive ancestral influence by inculcating in the pupils a proper reverence for the English connection, and proper deference for their social superiors, defined according to the exquisite English concept of class. The subsequent history of Ireland, and of the Irish abroad, however, suggests that the pupils proved too retarded to recognise their betters.

If the introduction of the state system in 1831 represented an important, though by no means revolutionary, contribution to primary education, subsequent developments lagged far behind those in Britain. Compulsory attendance introduced in England in 1870, with local option, was not extended to Ireland until 1892. In fact, attendance at private schools in Britain was higher than at state schools in Ireland even before the 1870 Act. The teaching profession was neglected in the most effective possible manner, through salaries averaging fifty per cent lower than in Britain – a disproportionate differential compared with the general relationship of professional and artisan incomes in the two countries – and through the inadequate provision of teacher training colleges. Not until 1883, when seventy per cent of the 11,000 teachers were still untrained, did adequate provision begin to be made for training colleges. By 1910, 1,276 teachers were being trained in eleven colleges.

Grudging though the state's contribution to primary education may have been, after the initiative of 1831, it far exceeded its contribution to secondary education. Until the Intermediate Education Act of 1878 Catholic secondary education, in contrast to the Protestant endowed schools, received no assistance from the state. Nevertheless, the number of Catholic secondary schools roughly trebled, from 20 to 60, between 1848 and 1879, thanks to the initiative of the religious orders. Without the unpaid devotion of the clergy secondary education for Catholics on this scale would have been impossible, for the remuneration of lay teachers would have made the fees prohibitive for the overwhelming majority of even middle-class Catholics. Even with the subsidy of unpaid clerical teaching, not many could afford the minimum £20 a year boarding fees – exceeding twenty per cent of the average clerk's income. Day schools, especially when run by the Christian Brothers, offered a better chance to lower middle-class children.

The intermediate system introduced in 1878 involved

centrally controlled external examinations of junior, middle and senior grades. Schools, irrespective of religion, were paid by results – extending a principle introduced in England in 1862 – with arts subjects, especially classics, initially priced higher than science subjects. The Act did not, however, greatly affect the trend rate of growth of secondary education. The number of pupils, which doubled from 5,000 in 1848 to 10,000 in 1878 did little more than double again, to about 20,000 in 1914, when ten per cent of the age group 15–18 were receiving secondary education.

In principle, the results system, by introducing impersonal, rational, specialised criteria into the assessment of academic merit in place of the traditional measuring rods of religion and sex, represented a major modernising achievement. The inclusion of girls' schools in the scheme somewhat stimulated female education, a modest milestone on the crawl towards equality of opportunity for women. Typically, however, the government was much more concerned with removing legal rather than economic barriers to equality. It refrained from making provision for scholarships to encourage the gifted poor among national school students to proceed to further education, thus ensuring that a substantial proportion of the £1 million it was spending annually by 1910 on primary education should be squandered. The provision of scholarships of one-tenth that value would have been, as A. P. Graves pointed out, 'so much intellectual soil reclaimed and saved from that melancholy process of going back to bog which is the order of the day'. Thomas O'Hagan, by now Lord Chancellor of Ireland, vice-President of the Intermediate Education Board and vice-Chancellor of the Royal University, reflected a lawyer's complacency concerning educational provision in assuring the Social Science Congress in 1881 that, as a result of the recent reforms 'the humblest in rank may reach the highest place in intellectual, and so, in social station . . . ability will have a full and fair career'. O'Hagan, still enveloped in the hallucinatory legal haze which had vitiated his predictions concerning the 1870 Land Act, remained oblivious to the fact that poverty precluded ninety per cent of Irish children from ever securing a toehold on the bottom rung of the secondary education ladder. This was no higher a proportion than in England, but it emphasises the fact that while the 1878 Act removed some minor obstacles to equality of educational opportunity it did little to remove the biggest obstacle of all, poverty.

The 'results system' has been frequently criticised for encouraging cramming and emphasising memory at the expense of intellect, thus producing an 'educated' class of mindless morons, immunised for life against the contagion of thought. Educational standards, however, measured by their capacity for fostering independence of mind, were generally mediocre before 1878. They did not deteriorate subsequently, but merely came to be administered by men whose quality of thinking itself reflected the poverty of the old system. In a results system, everything hinges on the criterion for gauging results. If examinations are intelligently conceived to demand evidence of independent thinking, then the results system will raise general receptivity to ideas. It was not the system, but the men who operated it, who condemned generations of students to the slow mental death which rendered them incapable of prescribing for the ills plaguing Irish society.

The condemnation by the hierarchy in 1850 of the Queen's Colleges established by Peel in 1845 in Belfast, Galway and Cork discouraged some Catholics from attending them, but simple lack of demand among provincial middle-class Catholics was probably a more important factor in restricting numbers. Newman's university, established in Dublin in 1854 as a Catholic alternative to Trinity College and the Queen's Colleges, never flourished. Lack of funds handicapped it from the outset. Much of the £190,000 spent was contributed by the pennies of the Catholic poor, fleeced to subsidise the education of middle-class Catholics. Conflicting concepts among the hierarchy of the role of a university also created problems, but the decisive weakness proved to be, again, lack of demand. The one faculty that flourished, medicine, in which the number of students rose from 36 in 1856 to over 300 in 1900, reflected the presence of an active market for medical education. The establishment of the Royal University in 1880 – modelled on London University – indirectly subsidised Catholic education by endowing an equal number of Catholic and Protestant Fellows. The government finally took the university question out of politics in 1908 by establishing the National University, modelled on the University of Wales.

Higher education probably made, on balance, a negative contribution to economic development before 1918. It was parasitic on the economy instead of constituting an ingredient of growth. This was not primarily because higher education was largely an export enclave, although no country in western Europe exported a comparable proportion of its graduates. It was not because the education was 'impractical'. Only in agriculture, admittedly an important exception, were the educational authorities at all levels reluctant to cater for the public demand for practical education. The model agricultural college at Glasnevin specialised in training its students out of Irish agriculture. Less than one-third of its graduates entered farming in Ireland. Its refresher courses for teachers were frequently farcical, their practical content consisting of little more than taking an occasional poke at a cow. The model schools throughout the country tended to be landlord hobbies, like that at Raphoe 'a capital botanical gardens, but there was no agriculture there'. On the rare occasions when the proposed education could be shown to bear some immediate relevance to Irish agriculture, public demand, as in the case of the establishment of the Cork dairy school in 1880, sufficed to overcome the hesitations of the authorities. Cork butter merchants and farmers, once convinced of the advantages of the proposal, were not amused by the impeccable antecedents of the argument of Sir Patrick Keenan, commissioner for national education, that 'it had never been done before, and he did not see why it should be done now'.

In other fields educators catered for the main mercenary chances on which students kept their eyes glued. Trinity College, for instance, created the first chair of civil engineering in the U.K. in 1844, as the railway building boom established a new academic field. A decade later Trinity proved so quick off the mark in training students for the Indian Civil Service examination that the *Saturday Review* was prompted to observe in 1858 that in replacing patronage by competition 'we are substituting Irishmen for Scotchmen in the Civil Government of India'. Medicine, which generally attracted the largest number of students in all colleges, was an uncompromisingly pocket profession. If business subjects roused little enthusiasm – in 1914–15 thirty-one per cent of students in University College, Dublin were reading medicine, only three per cent commerce – this was because many businessmen, as well as academics, were uninterested. The Dublin Chamber of Commerce, unlike its Belfast counterpart, had so few ideas on the subject of business education as late as 1902 that it decided not to present evidence before the Robertson Commission on university education.

Though poverty confined university education to a

derisory minority, the proportion was much the same as in western Europe in general. The number of students rose from 3,000 in 1871 to 4,000 in 1911, after dropping during the depression from 1877 to 1895. Those deprived of university education would, presumably, have aspired to become doctors, lawyers and divines. 'More of the same' would doubtless have made a considerable difference to the private fortunes of the individuals involved, but mattered little to the public welfare. The real problem was that in so far as university education inculcated intellectual attitudes towards economy and society, these proved at best irrelevant, at worst inimical, to Irish development. Signs of incipient change began to emerge towards the end of the century. T. J. Finlay and T. M. Kettle, early economics professors in the National University, showed themselves distinctly more alert to continental developments than the general run of Irish authorities. Even this growing awareness of the relevance of Europe to some extent reflected the crumbling of English complacency in the natural superiority of being British, as Germany, where the government played a more active role in economic life, overhauled her in several economic sectors.

Education, then, conforms to the requirements of the 'social laboratory' model to only a limited extent. In a host of other fields the areas where Ireland served as a laboratory were few and far between compared with those in which she lumbered along behind England. In virtually everything concerning urbanisation – in sanitation, housing, town planning – Ireland lagged. The two pillars of the modern British welfare state, the old age pensions Act of 1908 and the national insurance Act of 1911 owed their origins to a combination of English circumstances and German example. Bismarck did more than a century of Irish imbroglio to revise English concepts of the social and economic functions of the state.

The government's failure to stimulate economic growth was due more to intellectual irresponsibility than to political ill-will. Not the malevolence of the English mind, but the irrelevance of its preoccupations, impeded Irish progress. Because of its origins in private initiative the English industrial revolution helped create a climate of opinion which precluded the state initiatives that provided the only hope for sustained economic growth in Ireland. It was via this circuitous route rather than in the direct destruction of Irish industries that the industrial revolution exerted its most damaging influence on Ireland. The decline of rural industries became inevitable once the railway exposed the interior to competition. Local industries, like brewing and linen weaving, were sometimes destroyed by Dublin or Belfast competition. The problem was not why local firms collapsed, but why more of them were not destroyed by Irish instead of English manufacturers. The collapse of existing handicrafts was inevitable; the course of subsequent change was not. Due to lack of private enterprise this depended primarily on the nature of economic policy. But the overwhelming majority of state initiatives, and of the 'experts' contributions to the formulation of policy were frightening exercises in futility. However large government measures loom in studies of social and economic policy, they belong more to the intellectual history of England than to the economic history of Ireland. In practical terms, the government, the most powerful potential agent of economic development in Irish circumstances, simply opted out in obeisance to dogmas originally promulgated on the basis of English conditions. In the final analysis it was less the lack of mineral than of mental resources that inflicted on Ireland the slowest rate of growth of national income in western Europe, about 0·5 per cent per annum, between 1848 and 1914.

2   Land, Religion, Nationalism 1848–79

The Encumbered Estates Act

The famine years were pregnant with possibilities of long-term improvement, but to many contemporaries, landlords as well as tenants and labourers, they brought short-term disaster. Three immediate reactions reflected rival visions of the new Ireland that should arise on the grave of the old. Ironically, the one which aroused least contemporary interest eventually proved the most enduring. James Fintan Lalor's rebellion in Waterford in 1849 failed so farcically that few realised that there had even been an attempted movement to abolish landlordism and establish an independent Ireland. Well-informed contemporaries were preoccupied by the problem of the encumbered estates.

The decline of rents during the famine bankrupted over ten per cent of landlords. Lord John Russell's Whig government, convinced that a new breed of landlords would revitalise agriculture, seized the opportunity to pass the Encumbered Estates Act in 1849, after an abortive measure the previous year, simplifying procedures by which purchasers might acquire the forfeited estates. As Charles Wood, Chancellor of the Exchequer, put it 'I do not expect to see much improvement in Ireland till parties buy land for investment, meaning to improve it, and make it pay . . . at some number of years purchase capitalists will begin to buy, and then the reconstructing process begins'. Purchasers were indeed eager to buy at the early bargain prices, and about one-seventh of the country changed hands within a decade. But the purchasers were not the capitalists envisaged by Wood, whose prediction that experienced English farmers would flock across the Irish sea proved as fanciful as Pitt's fond belief fifty years earlier that the Union would induce English manufacturers to invest heavily in Ireland. Over ninety-five per cent of the five thousand purchasers were Irish, mainly younger sons of gentry, solicitors and shopkeepers who did well out of the famine.

Wood possessed one of the less gifted ministerial minds to apply itself to Irish affairs, but his absurd predictions should not be too severely censured, for he lacked reliable information on which to base policy. The agricultural statistics collected during the two preceding years, though incomparably superior to anything previously available, contained no direct information on investment patterns, which the Encumbered Estates Act was primarily intended to influence. The Act exerted little direct influence because the problems it was designed to solve did not generally exist. Agricultural change in the following decades owed much less to the Act than to price movements, which affected farmers under old and new landlords alike. Heavy investment in response to price changes – cattle numbers increased thirty-five per cent between 1847 and 1854, pigs and sheep one hundred and ten per cent, poultry fifty per cent – reflected an ample supply of agricultural capital. After 1850 over-investment in horses, important as status symbols, constituted a striking example of the mal-allocation of resources. In contrast to England no equine shortage hindered the tillage effort in the first World War, when acreage expanded nearly fifty per cent despite a virtually static number of horses.

The Act had, however, unintended consequences. The fact that the bulk of the purchasers, contrary to expectations, were Irish reduced absentee rents by about thirty per cent, if only by diverting them from England to Dublin, which received something of the tribute from rural Ireland lost after the Act of Union. By 1870 rents paid to landlords resident in Dublin exceeded those paid to absentees. The new landowners proved neither better nor worse agriculturalists or landlords than their predecessors. Rents, contrary to popular tradition, rarely rose spectacularly on their estates except for specific causes – where the coming of the railway increased the value of land, or where, especially in the far west, fragmented communal Rundale holdings were rearranged as private farms. Rents per acre (allowing for abatements during the famine) rose only marginally between 1848 and 1878, though rents per farm naturally rose as average farm sizes increased. The new landlords undoubtedly did well out of the Act, though not primarily through racking their tenants, but simply because of the bargain prices at which they bought. The Act did not release a horde of predatory new landlords on a defenceless tenantry. It was, however, highly significant that the old landlords acquired a mellow retrospective glow – once they had been safely bought out. Critics who compared new landlords unfavourably with their predecessors carefully refrained from singing the praises of the surviving old landlords, still masters of six-sevenths of the country in 1860. That the distinction should be drawn emphasised the incipient distintegration of the deferential pre-famine social structure. The casting of the estates old into another mould eroded traditional loyalties. If title to land could be so simply transferred, why might it not be transferred to the tenant rather than to a new, frequently far from noble, purchaser? Why not every tenant his own landlord? The Encumbered Estates Act played a significant role in stimulating tenant thought about the structure of property rights in land,

and contributed to the revolution in historical consciousness which allowed many farmers to be convinced
a generation later that they, as the rightful heirs of the
despoiled celtic landowners and not the landlords, were
the legitimate owners of the land, a revelation granted
to few as early as 1849.

The Tenant League

Such subversive sentiments were certainly far from the
minds of most supporters of the third solution proffered
to the problems of 1849. After some abortive attempts to
form tenant associations in the south in 1847 and 1848
two Catholic curates, Shea and O'Keeffe, succeeded in
organising a tenant protection society in Callan, Co.
Kilkenny, in October 1849. Twenty similar societies
were established by July 1850. In August three journalists,
Charles Gavan Duffy, the Young Irelander, Sir John
Grey of the *Freeman's Journal,* and Frederick Lucas, the
English Catholic convert editor of the *Tablet,* founded
a national Tenant League Association to achieve the
'3 Fs', fair rent, fixity of tenure and free sale.

The rise and fall of the Tenant League reflects the
still limited nature of rural participation in mass social
movements. The southern tenant associations did not
arise as a direct response to famine. They represented the
reaction of the prosperous, market-orientated wheat and
barley growers, who suffered relatively little in the famine
itself, but were severely affected by the thirty-five per
cent fall in wheat prices aggravated by poor yields
between 1847 and 1849. Whereas wheat accounted for
only twenty-two per cent of the national grain crop in
1849, it contributed over forty-five per cent of the total
grain acreage in Kilkenny and Tipperary, the most
active centres of Tenant League activity. The Callan
association was formed immediately after a particularly
poor wheat harvest, and the even more disastrous harvest

of 1850, when Leinster yields fell a further thirty per cent, intensified discontent. The very fact that Tenant Leagues appealed primarily to 'a class of respectable and sturdy farmers who were possessed of competent means'[1] doomed the League from the outset. In view of the strata involved, it was no wonder that fewer than five per cent of their delegates to the national conference in August 1850 came from west of a line running from Cork to Derry. The fact that the grain farmers were responding more to short-term cyclical depression than to basic feelings concerning the fundamental injustice of the land system ensured that once the depression passed their agitational ardour would cool. Confronted by falling wheat and barley prices in the late 1840s they switched exceptionally rapidly to livestock. Low grain prices persisted until 1853, when the Crimean War brought a sixty per cent surge in wheat prices and forty per cent in barley prices. Grain yields in the south-east simultaneously climbed fifty per cent above the 1850 trough, effectively undermining the whole basis of agitation.

The Tenant League did not, however, consist exclusively of the larger eastern grain farmers. Parliament's rejection of William Sharman Crawford's Bill to legalise the Ulster Custom, which allowed an evicted tenant to sell his occupation right to the highest bidder, awakened Ulster tenants to their precarious legal position if landlords wished to evict. The Presbyterian clergy seized on this threat to rouse their farmer flocks against Anglican landlords. The Tory press, which had already hastened to instruct the retarded natives in the niceties of political etiquette by denouncing tenant right priests as 'half starved dogs', need not however, have become so hysterical about the threat posed by 'that monstrous coalition between the Romish priesthood and the communism of other creeds' because the growing identification throughout 1851 of the southern tenant leagues with

Catholic demands provoked the withdrawal of the north-east.

The Independent Irish party

An outbreak of No-Popery swept England in 1851 when the Pope assigned English territorial titles to Catholic bishops. In an impressive display of national solidarity Lord John Russell's Whig government passed the Ecclesiastical Titles Act, forbidding Catholic clerics to assume such titles and banning the wearing of religious habits. Patriotic natives sacked Catholic churches, leading to remonstrations with Irish settlers, most conspicuously at Stockport. With religious fervour at fever pitch a Catholic Defence Association, established in Ireland in 1851 acquired the support of several M.P.s who came to be known as the Irish Brigade. About 40 of the 48 Brigade supporters returned in the July 1852 general election formed themselves into the Independent Irish Party in September, pledged to oppose any English party which did not repeal the Ecclesiastical Titles Act and adopt the Tenant League programme. However, the religious aspects lost for the League such residual Presbyterian sympathy as may have lingered, and the Brigade failed to secure a solitary seat in Ulster. As the election left the Independent Party holding the balance of power in the House of Commons it helped bring down Derby's Tory government when it rejected their land reform bill. In Aberdeen's new Whig administration, formed in December 1852, however, two independent members, John Sadleir and William Keogh, broke their pledge by taking office. Sadleir and Keogh rank among the most remarkable Irishmen of the century. Sadleir, the enterprising founder of the Tipperary Bank indulged in swindles of epic proportions. Keogh, a convivial careerist, won many recruits to the nationalist cause by his vitriolic harangues of political prisoners from the bench. Despite their rare talents, the loss of the two members did not spell ruin for the party. Much more important was the decline in tenant interest once agricultural prices revived in 1853, and the decline in episcopal support when the No-Popery eruption subsided. Even these weaknesses could have been surmounted by resolute leadership, for the bishops were merely neutral, not hostile. But the League lacked leaders of real stature. Frederick Lucas, unable to arouse the popular support which would compel the bishops to follow in its wake, could think of no alternative but to vainly appeal to the Pope to censure alleged episcopal hostility to the League in 1854. Gavan Duffy emigrated in despair to Australia in 1855, Lucas died the same year. The suicide of Sadleir when his swindles were discovered in 1856 – never in Irish history did so few owe so much to so many – retrieved some wavering support among those impressed with such revelations of divine displeasure, but the new leader, George Henry Moore, was unseated in 1857 because of the distinctly terrestrial nature of the clerical influence which helped secure his election in Mayo. The rump of the party split up the centre over the interpretation of its oath in 1858, and faded into oblivion.

Cardinal Cullen's Church

Lucus and Duffy liked to attribute the ignominious decline of the Independent Irish Party to the malevolent influence of Paul Cullen, who returned from Rome to become archbishop of Armagh in 1849 before being translated to Dublin in 1852. Fenians and Unionists likewise considered him the main bane of Irish public life in his generation. 'Ungenial recluse', 'hard Italian monk', 'implacable Churchman', 'relentless prelate', were among the kinder epithets hurled by critics at this remarkable man. The *Times* dismissed all his pastorals for 'palpable ignorance, puerility and utter absence even of the marks of ordinary education', and, in as monumental a mis-judgement as a Fenian propagandist ever passed on the prelate, thundered 'had Doctor Cullen a single idea of his own in his head, did he know an atom more than he does, had he any natural perception of truth, could he write a word of English he would be wholly unfit to have a position of chief pastor of Romish Ireland. As it is, without one independent thought, or the capacity for one, without one particle of knowledge, even theological, but of what he obtained in the seminary lecture room from some convenient summary of the tridentine catechism, with an understanding exactly on a level with that of his flock by simply reflecting an Irish standard of everything, he is as convenient a tool of Irish faction, as can possibly be found and is the very man to be the Irish religious leader and authority'.

Cullen, who became rector of the Irish College in Rome in 1831, at the age of 29, retained throughout life the character of the headmaster of the Irish Church. The personal contacts he established with the Vatican bureauc-racy during eighteen years in Rome, a feline sensitivity for the levers of power in the Vatican, a strong, subtle, if narrow intelligence, a fusion of flexible tactics with consistent strategy, and sheer longevity – he reigned from 1849 till 1878 – enabled him to stamp a deep imprint on the Catholic Church in Ireland and to acquire sufficient international stature to be created Ireland's first Cardinal in 1866 and play a prominent role in the Vatican Council in 1870.

Cullen considered himself merely the Pope's chief whip in Ireland. In other circumstances he might indeed have been an outstanding party organiser, a powerful machine boss. He whipped the Church into line with Roman discipline, initially at the synod of Thurles in 1850, which tightened ecclesiastical discipline and intro-duced greater uniformity into religious observances, and subsequently through witch hunts which winkled out deviationists who insisted that the authority of a General Council derived 'not so much from the confirmation of the Supreme Pontiff as from the majority vote of the Bishops'. The submission in 1855 of Professor Crolly of Maynooth 'who signed a most humble retraction expressing his regret for what he had done, withdrawing opinions which he had expressed and promising to do everything possible to mitigate the scandal which he had given' symbolised the triumph of ultramontanism over Gallicanism.

Cullen transformed the Irish Church from a Latin-American type institution into one of the most efficiently marshalled Churches in Europe. Despite initial opposition – in 1853 Cullen complained that the decrees of the synod of Thurles were ignored in Thurles itself – by 1878 few priests of the vintage described by Archbishop Croke as 'excellent, but fully 82 years of age, a man who does not believe in missions, confraternities, domiciliary visits, frequent confessions or anything of the sort' were left to disturb the Cullen vision of Catholic Ireland as a vast mission field.

Cullen's austere dedication to the primacy of merit largely stamped out nepotism within the Church. He adhered to the principles he emphasised in counselling against the appointment of a certain Fr McDermott as Dean to Bishop Gillooly 'I know the claims of his family and I would most willingly do anything in my power to oblige the O'Connors but where the interests of the Church at large are at stake we must look to the personal merits of every candidate'. His bishops – and the Vatican frequently followed his advice on appointments instead of that of the priests of the dioceses involved – tended to be scholars and monks, strangers to the dioceses rather than convivial local parish priests. Ironically, the centralising policy of Cullen, the ultramontane, did more to break down local boundaries and accustom the faithful to think in national terms than did the attitude of his Gallican opponents like Archbishop MacHale of Tuam, for Gallican in the Irish context meant the cherishing less of national than of merely local customs.

The Catholic secondary school system is largely his creation. He introduced a host of teaching orders to cater for all classes of Catholics. But in fostering the creation of an educated Catholic bourgeoisie – both Blackrock and Terenure were founded in 1860 – Cullen never neglected the poor. He strongly encouraged the Christian Brothers schools, which provided virtually the only hope of secondary education for poor children. No Irish public figure of his generation championed so consistently the rights of the urban poor as this son of a prosperous farmer. He consistently objected to conventional official calumnies concerning the nature of poverty, censuring the managers of the Poor Law who 'treat poverty as a crime to be dealt with more severely than robbery and murder'. The plight of the poor was the most insistent theme running through his pastorals and private writings, and he despised 'fashionable' English Catholics, determined to atone for Christ's appalling gaffe in having consented to be born in a manger by aping the Anglican attitude towards churches as genteel plutocratic parlours instead as houses of worship where sceptre and spade were equal made. His emphasis on the church building as the centre of worship, apart from stimulating a building boom, permitted participation in services very lax before the famine, if only because of lack of accommodation, to increase sharply. The emphasis on the physical primacy of the church buildings concentrated the specialised functions hitherto diffused as status symbols among the private homes of the more affluent members of the community, who suffered with ill-concealed chagrin Cullen's insistence on the equality of Catholics before God.

Although nationalists bitterly criticised his behaviour, and although he constantly opposed violence, Cullen was the antithesis of a 'castle Catholic'. One of his first decisions when translated to Dublin in 1852 was not to attend Castle levees. Frederick Lucas' own account of his interview with Cullen in Rome on 24 January 1855 places the issues involved in the archbishop's attitude to the Independent Irish Party in clear perspective: 'On the part to be taken by priests in politics he (Cullen) said the business of a priest was to confine himself to his spiritual duties and in the intervals of these to confine himself to reading and meditation; but if the Church was attacked in such a way that all Catholics must agree upon it, then they should come out; but wherever two Catholics might differ then they should take no part lest by doing so they should get into collision with one part of their flock; that with regard to elections they ought to tell the people their duty to avoid bribery and perjury and to vote for a candidate favourable to the Church; if a candidate avowedly hostile to the Church showed himself they might warn the people against him, though with caution; but if two candidates presented themselves both not professing sentiments hostile to the Church, their business was not to interfere between them but to stick to general principles.

Monsignor Talbot turned to me and asked if I concurred. I said that on the contrary I entirely dissented and that the practical meaning of such a course was to hand over the constituency in a very short time to the enemies of the Church and the people'.

Lucas' objection to 'the practical meaning' of Cullen's attitude carries some force, but only because Lucas lacked the leadership capacity to create a lay political alternative to the priests' electioneering role. That was to come, however, more rapidly than Lucas foresaw. Cullen reserved the right to decide what 'avowedly hostile to the Church' meant, but he basically conceded the autonomy of politics from religion. And he practised what he preached. The first priests he reprimanded for over-zealous political activity were actually opponents of the Tenant League.

Cullen was a great organiser. But it would be a mistake to dismiss him as merely an archetypal *apparatchik*. His insistence on the authority of bishops over priests, 'a bishop must *govern*' and of the Pope over the bishops, his ostentatious fidelity to Pius IX, tend to conceal the fact that while he spoke with his master's voice on matters of internal Church discipline he held firm independent views concerning the role of the Church in society. For Cullen was a liberal Catholic. In contrast to Pius IX he almost invariably used the term 'liberal' as a term of praise. His discreet ignoring of the injunctions of the Syllabus of Errors of 1864, which denounced the separation of Church and State as a sign of Satan's presence in an infidel modern world, was not wholly dictated by the fact that the Church to be separated in the Irish context was a Protestant Church. Cullen worked towards disestablishment long before Gladstone conceded it in 1869, but he rejected the scheme of 'concurrent endowment' which, instead of disestablishing the Church of Ireland, proposed to establish the Catholic Church alongside it. Cullen opted for the principle of a free Church in a free State, for no established Churches rather than for two. After early hysterical outbursts – 'the devil who animates Protestantism does not hold himself obliged to observe any promise', Cullen calmed down as the threat from Protestant activity receded after the immediate post-famine depression. He remained a master of theological double think – Catholic 'missionaries' win 'converts', Protestant 'proselytisers' win 'perverts'. But in recommending Catholics in 1857 'to vote concientiously for honest and upright men, men of religion and principle, who will not be indifferent to the destitution of the poor in our workhouses, men who will protect the rights of the working classes and defend the rights of religion' Cullen readily acknowledged that 'there are many such men of every creed; there are Protestants whom no consideration would induce to injure the Catholic religion and Catholics who respect the feelings of Protestants'.

Cullen's clergy did not, of course, preach an explicit gospel of modernisation. Nor should he himself be considered a conscious missionary of modernisation. But his determination to assert the primacy of merit over birth, to mobilise the masses, to emphasise the specialisation of roles within the Church and of the role of the Church itself in society contributed to the creation of systematic sustained participation in institutional religion. This represented a basic change from the 'peasant revolt' syndrome of previous participatory religious movements, sudden but ephemeral outbursts punctuating general apathy. Some of Cullen's achievements would have distressed him had he appreciated them. Despite his own distaste for exhibitionism his church building programme helped foster the consumer consciousness it was partly intended to curb. The 'Sunday suit' or the 'Sunday shawl' became obligatory, for the rags that had sufficed in many of the pre-famine churches seemed out of place in the fine new buildings. At a more profound level, while Cullen's Church helped mould new participatory personalities, these reacted selectively to the specific doctrines preached. Cullen might rank 'the sin of drunkeness' with 'the sin of impurity' as 'peculiarly offensive to Almighty God' but his flock exercised their discretion, at least publicly, in the matter. His policy contributed to stimulating the masses to become a public opinion, but that public opinion decisively rejected his own political initiatives.

Cullen's achievement becomes even more remarkable in view of the temptations which beset him. Given a virtual *tabula rasa* on which to carve his own design, he might have led the Irish Church in a genuinely theocratic direction, adopting the uncompromising ideological attitude of his doughty French ultramontane contemporary, Bishop Pié. Instead he responded positively to the challenge of change, whether in the field of Church-State relations or in supporting rather than censuring economic development. He directed the clergy's energy to their spiritual mission, attempted to limit their political and social role, acknowledged the independence of the secular from the sacred, and displayed almost consistent common sense and moderation. He followed O'Connell's permissive dictum 'our religion from Rome, our politics from Ireland'. That Irish Catholicism, the most piously popular religion in northern Europe, eschewed the spirit of the Syllabus of Errors and remained politically pragmatic must be partly attributed to the guidance of Paul the Prudent.

Orangeism

The suppression of the Orange Order in 1835 had as little effect in moderating Orange ardour as the suppression of the Catholic Association had on Catholic fervour in the 1820s. Principles cannot be suppressed as simply as institutions. The *Freeman's Journal* concluded from the relatively restrained celebration of 12 July 1850 that the tenant leagues had at last curbed landlord influence over the Protestant tenantry, and thus led to 'the decay of those insane feuds which had been perpetuated by and for the landlord party . . . time and reason have done it, and both will extend it until a common union indissolubly binds every class of Irishmen, and presents for the first time in our history an equalised and compact people'. The *Freeman's* optimism proved somewhat premature. As recently as 12 July 1849, the killing of about 20 Catholics in a skirmish at Dolly's Brae attested to the enduring intensity of sectarian loyalties, which continued to be reflected in such humble cases, barely worth a passing press mention, as that of one Gillespie, an ex-army sergeant, who 'had gone into a house where an Orange Lodge was held and had said, in a joke, that he was "a papist", which he was not: and he was consequently attacked and lost his life'.[2] The Orange sense of humour would baffle wishful thinkers of the *Freeman* variety for some time to come.

Minor disturbances occurred nearly every 12 July in Belfast during the 1850s. The historic significance of the 1857 riots, which claimed an unknown number of victims, was that they marked the definitive urbanisation of ancestral rural animosities. Between 1841 and 1851, as famine refugees flocked into Belfast, the number of immigrants rose from 17,000 to 43,000, from twenty-three to forty-three per cent of the population. Belfast, hitherto relatively free from sectarian strife, now became the prisoner of Ulster's rural past. 'Respectable' citizens still tended to maintain their distance from vulgar Orangeism, but to dismiss the Order at this period as 'a mere working class movement' overlooks the fact that by taking firm root among the most rapidly growing sector of the population, Orangeism consolidated a crucial constituency. However much their natural leaders failed them, the instinct of the Protestant people has always remained unerring.

Archbishop Cullen sounded an apparently hysterical note in denouncing in March 1857 'the bigoted fanatical proselytising Orange faction, a faction hostile to every liberal Protestant no less than to everything Catholic. They are anxious to repeal the Catholic Emancipation Act, to exclude every Catholic from even the lowest office, to raise a clamour if any Catholic receives the reward of his talents . . .' Yet, within a few months the Rev. Dr Thomas Drew, Grand Chaplain to the Orange Order, vindicated the gravamen of Cullen's charge.

Drew displayed an impressive command of the dialectic in translating the lessons of the Sermon on the Mount, which served as 'an everlasting rebuke to all intolerance, and of legislative and ecclesiastical cruelty' into practical terms. Catholic Emancipation should be repealed, and all Catholics expelled from parliament, for a monopoly of state jobs formed part of 'the true Protestant birthright'. 'To be a Protestant in Ireland is a positive disqualification', he thundered, unveiling the secrets of his private statistical service, for 'the chief places of justice, and the many offices in the state, customs and excise, and foreign departments are assigned to Romanists' – at a time when just one-third of the judgeships and not a single other higher legal office, and just half the appointments in the customs and excise branches were held by Catholics! He dismissed the rather widespread belief that Ireland was a predominantly Catholic country on the grounds that the official census was a conspiracy: 'by reason of a falsified census the numbers of the Protestants were set down vastly below their real amount'. He showed little patience for the modern tendency to apply secular criteria to secular life. The mission of the United Kingdom was 'to aim at Protestantising the world', which involved 'a certain test of men and their conduct . . . this book is well written, very clever, very fascinating, but has it testified for Protestantism? This newspaper is ably edited: does it breathe a Protestant spirit? This lecture is enter-taining on stones, on shells, birds, beasts, political economy, and philosophical discoveries: what does he say for God and the soul, truth and Protestantism'. [3]

The unhelpful evidence of the census of 1861, recording 4·5 million Catholics compared with 700,000 Episcopalians and 600,000 others, counselled the silent abandonment of

Drew's flights of statistical fancy. Instead, Protestants fell back on the simpler argument that numbers didn't much matter because of the natural inferiority of Catholics. To the Rev. A. Hume, author of the most detailed exegesis of the census, Protestants were 'the cream of the Irish milkpot', the cream, being, apparently, twice as thick as the milk, for Hume considered one million Protestants the equivalent of about two million Catholics.

The incredulous commissioners of enquiry into the 1857 riots noted the familiar ingredients that have kept the pot on the boil ever since. They condemned the partisan local police, almost exclusively Protestant, many themselves Orangemen, recommending that 'a total change be effected in the mode of appointment and the management of the local police in Belfast'. They sharply criticised, through the uncomprehending eyes of modern men, the manner of the celebration of the 12 July: 'the revolution of 1688, founding as it did free institutions for the benefit of every class and creed, might be commemorated by all: but unfortunately its commemoration is now regarded in the North of Ireland as the celebration of the triumph of one class over another, and the establishment of Protestant ascendancy: and it is entirely forgotten, that the principles of the revolution are, in fact, the principles of civil and religious liberty'.[4] In 1857 Belfast decisively emerged as a major paradox – rapidly industrialising, yet doggedly defying the pressures of the modernisation process. Religion became the opium of the working classes in their struggle for status and jobs. Industrialisation and urbanisation, providing the only hope that the rural roots of prejudice might wither away, became instead powerful agencies for the perpetuation and accentuation of sectarian animosity. It was grimly symbolic that the shipyards, cynosures of the new industrial age, should become the most militant custodians of traditional loyalties. Three hundred ships' carpenters 'armed with thick and sharp edged staves, used for building vessels' formed the bodyguard of the Reverend 'Roaring' Hugh Hanna, a Presbyterian preacher who defied the magistrates by beginning open-air preaching in the hitherto 'non-sectarian' centre of Belfast, and thus sparked off the riots for which he denied any responsibility on the grounds that 'our most valuable rights have been obtained by conflict: if we cannot maintain them without that, we must submit to the necessity'. The 1857 riots marked the decisive turning point when Ulster history failed to turn, when Belfast missed the final entry to the modernisation highway and continued to grind relentlessly around the traditional track for the rest of the century.

Fenianism

Little did Cullen realise, as he penned ritual denunciations of ribbonism and freemasonry into his pastoral for St Patrick's Day 1858, that a greater than these was about to come among his flock, for on that 17 March the Fenians were founded. The Irish in America were anxious to express their hostility to England in institutional form. The natural leader of such a movement was John Mitchel, who escaped from Tasmania in 1853 and seemed destined to revitalise the revolutionary movement. But Mitchel, a propagandist, not an organiser, subordinated his devotion to the sacred causes of Irish unity and Irish freedom to the equally sacred causes of American partition and negro slavery. It was not until St Patrick's Day 1858 that two dimmer 1848 lights, Michael Doheny and John O'Mahony, officially inaugurated the new, as yet anonymous, movement in New York. Emissaries from Doheny and O'Mahony had established contact with another 1848 veteran, James Stephens, on his return to Ireland from Paris in 1856. Stephens agreed to organise a movement in Ireland, provided the Irish Americans placed adequate funds at his disposal and acknowledged him as provisional dictator of the organisation. Adequate funds were never, in fact, forthcoming, and the 400 dollars with which the conspirators launched the movement were a long maturing investment. Stephens proved a superb recruiter, even if he fussily insisted on creating the organisation in the image of the ludicrously elaborate secret societies with which he came into contact in Paris, offering maximum opportunity to informers. The organisation, riddled with spies, could no more hold its secrets than a sieve could hold water. The most distinguished of Stephens' early recruits was O'Donovan Rossa, a founder of the Phoenix Society in Skibbereen in 1856, which merged into Stephens' movement.

The organisation, soon known as the Irish Republican Brotherhood, combined a demand for total separation from England, achieved, if necessary, by physical force with a visceral, if loosely defined, commitment to agrarian reform. The proclamation of the Fenian Provisional Government in 1867 asserted that 'our rights and liberties have been trampled on by an alien aristocracy, who, treating us as foes, usurped our lands, and drew away from our unfortunate country all material riches . . . today, having no honourable alternative left, we again appeal to force as a last resort . . . unable longer to endure the curse of monarchical government, we aim at founding a Republic based on universal suffrage, which shall secure to all the intrinsic value of their labour. The soil of Ireland at present in the possession of an oligarchy belongs to us, the Irish people, and to us it must be restored. We declare, also, in favour of absolute liberty of conscience, and the complete separation of Church and State . . . we intend no war against the people of England; our war is against the aristocratic locusts whether English or Irish, who have eaten the verdure of our fields'. Most Fenian leaders supported peasant proprietorship, but preferred on tactical grounds to postpone the formulation of specific plans for social reform until after independence.

The funeral of Terence Bellew McManus, 10 November 1861, indicated the depth of the potential reservoir of support on which the Fenians could draw. In some respects the funeral signalled a turning point in the history of Irish public opinion. McManus, another 1848 veteran, died in America, and his funeral procession, first in Cork, then in Dublin, demonstrated for the first time massive public sympathy for the spirit of Young Ireland. In contrast to 1848, when revolutionaries mustered little sympathy, never mind support, several thousand people defied Cullen's displeasure to salute the spirit of rebellion only thirteen years after the fiasco of Ballingarry.

A. M. Sullivan, leader of the moderate constitutional nationalists whose ambition to claim the coffin for themselves Stephens thwarted, concluded that the funeral 'gave the Fenian chiefs a command of Ireland which they had not been able to command before'. But not even Fenians can live by funerals alone. The agricultural crisis from 1860 to 1863 powerfully reinforced the Fenian appeal. The number of holdings, which increased from 555,000 in 1853 to 568,000 in 1861, fell to 546,000 by 1867. The decline in the number of cows and pigs increased the vulnerability of the dairying areas to Fenian propaganda. Recruitment increased encouragingly among agricultural labourers and in the British army, where John Devoy followed Ribbon precedent in recruiting soldiers, and among building workers and shop clerks in Dublin and Cork, a disproportionate number of whom were first generation rural migrants who found in Fenianism the cameraderie that helped integrate them into their new urban environment.

Stephens, sensing the size of potential public support, became increasingly impatient with the miserable trickle of money from America – only £1,500 between 1858 and 1864. His decision to found a newspaper, *The Irish People*, in November 1863 increased friction between himself and O'Mahony, who disapproved of the organisation coming out into the open. The internal dissensions provoked O'Mahony to depose Stephens to be mere 'representative for Europe' and have himself elected head centre by the American organisation. With the end of the American Civil War in 1865, the Fenians sought to enlist thousands of experienced Irish soldiers and officers. But the continuing failure of America to send arms or money prevented Stephens from fulfilling his promise that 1865 would be the year of insurrection. The government, copiously informed of Fenian plans by spies, pounced on the offices of *The Irish People* in September 1865 and arrested the leaders. Stephens soon escaped from Richmond prison to America, where, apart from displacing O'Mahony, he did little to fulfil his revised promise that 1866 would be the year of revolution, Irish-American officers deposed him in December and sent Colonels Kelly and Massey, two civil war veterans, to Ireland. Massey was captured, but Kelly managed to inject some urgency into proceedings. After an isolated February flare-up near Kenmare, the insurrection fizzled out in floods of rain and recriminations as the capricious elements doused the attempted risings on 5 March 1867. A scatter of skirmishes, most notably at Tallaght, notching a total of twelve fatalities, less than a self-respecting Belfast riot could boast, appeared to be the total outcome of all the scheming and organising, elections and depositions, hopes and fears of a decade's hard labour. But the significance lay in the sequel. Colonel Kelly was arrested in Manchester in September. Three Fenians, Allen, Larkin, and O'Brien were enthusiastically hanged for accidentally killing a policeman in the attempt to rescue Kelly from the prison van. The execution of the 'Manchester Martyrs' roused Irish public opinion to extraordinary fervour. T. D. Sullivan wrote 'God save Ireland', which served as the national anthem for fifty years, and the 23 November, the 'feast' of the 'martyrs' soon superseded St Patrick's Day as the national political feastday.

Fenianism was the first nationwide lay secular society. No previous movement in Irish history, Catholic or Protestant, relied so little on clerical support. Not only was the leadership completely lay, but it came from a distinctly more plebian level than the leadership of any earlier movement. Whatever John O'Leary's aristocratic pretentions, or John O'Mahony's family vanity, the key men in the movement, Stephens himself, a civil engineer, O'Donovan Rossa, an evicted farmer's son who became a grocer, Edward Duffy, another farmer's son who became a shop assistant, John Nolan a commercial traveller who organised Fenianism in Belfast, John Devoy, a cottier's son, sprang from different social strata, felt instinctively in different social terms, than the Young Ireland leaders. They harboured no fear of peasant revolt. Unlike the Young Irelanders, whose influence never spread far beyond Dublin, and whose effort to rouse the country in 1848 was, as the *Kilkenny Journal* rightly observed, 'an attempt to find the fruits of the prurient eloquence of the clubrooms among a generous but ill-instructed peasantry, few of whom had ever heard the names of the orators', Stephens and Rossa prowled the country for recruits. Stephens' tireless tramping earned him the sobriquet 'an seabhac siulach' – the wandering hawk. Fenianism was the first political movement to channel the energies of agricultural labourers and small farmers, hitherto expressed in ribbonism and faction fighting, into a national organisation. By permeating local discontents with a national perspective the Fenians, like their great enemy in the ecclesiastical sphere, Cardinal Cullen, helped broaden petty horizons and foster a sense of national political consciousness. Fenianism served as a school for sedition for the next generation. 'Ex-Fenians' played an active role in the Home Rule movement, raising the threshold level of constitutional demands and infusing constitutional politics with a vigour and determination largely lacking hitherto.

The Fenian break-through into new areas was as significant as their mobilisation of new classes. Perhaps the most important feature of O'Donovan Rossa's Phoenix Society was its location, in west Cork, hitherto largely untouched by revolutionary movements. The growth of Fenian support in the south-west initiated a significant extension which presaged the general location of the war of independence from 1919 to 1921. The driving force of Fenian support in these areas was the memory of the famine. Skibbereen suffered severely from its ravages, and O'Donovan Rossa's first recorded speech, in 1858, developed the theme that the famine was neither of infernal nor divine, but human origin. Fenianism began the grassroots revolt against the fatalism, so reassuring to the official mind, which drove thousands to their famine graves. Connacht remained the least organised province, but Fenianism drew it appreciably closer to the main stream of national political consciousness. The tour of Connacht by O'Donovan Rossa and Ned Duffy in 1864, which sowed the seeds that were to sprout fifteen years later in the Land League, marks the beginning of the modernisation of western mentalities.

The Fenian insurrection failed for want of arms and effective military leadership. An insurrection could not hope for success, irrespective of whether it occurred in 1865 or 1867, against a professional military enemy, without a far greater supply of arms and military expertise from America. Even had the movement escaped internal dissensions, badly armed amateurs could not hope for success against trained killers. Episcopal condemnation exerted little influence on Fenian fortunes. Some potential supporters may have been deterred by clerical condemnation, but it was not numbers, but expertise, the Fenians lacked. Ironically, the main outbreaks in 1867, at Tallaght and Kenmare, occurred in the dioceses of the most resolute episcopal opponents of Fenianism, Cullen and Moriarty.

Justice for Ireland

Cullen, a moderate nationalist opposed in principle to physical force, supported a rival organisation, the National Association, established in 1864 to channel public enthusiasm into constitutional channels. The Association turned out to be a calm in a tea cup. Among prominent Catholic laymen only John Blake Dillon adhered to it for any length of time. Dr Norman, a leading authority on the Association, suggests that its main mistake was to dissipate its energies on three aims, disestablishment of the Church of Ireland, a Catholic University, and a mild measure of land reform, instead of concentrating on a single objective. It is less than self-evident, however, that any of the three issues, taken singly or collectively, roused much public enthusiasm. The Association, all officers and no soldiers, never acquired sufficient popular support to transform it into a mass movement, to translate it out of the ecclesiastical parlours into the fields. It had difficulty in raising even £500 in 1865. Its failure to strike a responsive chord in the public mind cannot be attributed to the lack of local organisation, or to its virtually exclusive Dublin orientation. The Home Rule by-election successes between 1871 and 1873 showed that a national organisation could follow rather than precede the capture of the country if spontaneous grassroots support existed. The fact that the bishops themselves went behind the Association's back in abortive negotiation on the university question between 1865 and 1868 indicated how little they rated its influence. Gladstone's programme in 1868 did coincide with that of the Association – disestablishment, university reform, land reform. But it was the Fenians who concentrated Gladstone's attention on Ireland. Any English statesman wishing to 'do something' for Ireland inevitably turned to the staple problems of religion, education and land; and Gladstone did not in fact wholly adopt the Association's programme. He fully accepted it on disestablishment, partly on land, and not at all on education.

When the Liberals gained ten seats at the general election of 1868 it seemed that a union of hearts had been established between constitutional nationalism and English liberalism. But disestablishment dominated the election – Presbyterian support gained the Liberals three seats in Ulster – and it would be an excessively Hibernian mode of argument to claim that the Irish party system had been wholly integrated into that of the U.K., and the union finally made to work, when the prime reason for supporting the Liberals was to remove a prop of the union. Disestablishment was largely a symbolic issue, but it did mark a step in the official modernisation of the state in so far as it conferred formal equality of opportunity on the rival religions.

The Land Act of 1870 legalised the Ulster Custom where it existed. It stipulated that tenants should receive compensation for improvements, if evicted for non-payment of rent, and 'compensation for disturbance' if evicted for any other reason. The Act was well intentioned, but neither Gladstone nor his critics understood Irish agriculture. The statistics collected since 1847 lend little support to the widespread contemporary conviction that the Ulster Custom made a significant contribution to the alleged superiority of Ulster agriculture, and that security of tenure provided the solution to improving Irish agriculture. Contemporaries measured the influence of the Ulster

Custom according to social instead of economic criteria – from the fact that fewer agrarian outrages occurred in the North. The Ulster Custom contributed greatly to peace and quiet, but made little difference to the economic performance of Northern agriculture, which was not, in fact, more efficient than that of the South. Throughout the period wheat yields remained slightly higher than the national average in the North, but oats and barley yields fell further behind, and potato yields remained virtually identical. Likewise, relative livestock densities remained largely unchanged. The decline in tillage acreage and the rise in livestock numbers proceeded at much the same pace north and south, irrespective of tenurial customs, after 1847. Northern and southern farmers reacted similarly to the same stimuli, indicating the irrelevance of tenure arrangements to the economics, as distinct from the sociology, of rural Ireland. Gladstone's first land Act therefore had no economic, and indeed few social, consequences. As the bulk of evictions occurred for non-payment of rent, the 'compensation for disturbance' clause, however revolutionary in English theory in recognising the tenant's right to an interest in his holding, made little difference in Irish practice.

University education was the third sphere in which Gladstone attempted to secure 'justice for Ireland'. He proposed to establish a new university in Dublin, which would include a Catholic college as well as Trinity College. This failed to satisfy either the Trinity authorities, unwilling to be associated with a Catholic institution, or the Catholic hierarchy infuriated by the lack of financial support from the state for the proposed new college. The bishops influenced the Irish Liberals to vote against the measure in 1873 and thereby helped bring about the resignation of the government.

When Gladstone refused an amnesty for the Fenian prisoners, grassroots opinion turned rapidly against him in Ireland. The Amnesty Association, organised by a Fenian, John Nolan, roused considerable popular support. By March 1869 subscriptions were averaging £40 a week. The Tipperary by-election in November 1869 dramatically illustrated the precarious nature of the Liberal electoral base. O'Donovan Rossa, by then a prisoner in Millbank Jail, stood as an unrepentent Fenian, the first felon to face an electoral test in Irish history. The circumstances were highly unpromising. It was little over two years since the ignominious failure of the rising, a year since the greatest electoral triumph of the Liberal Party in Irish history, a few months since disestablishment. Rossa's liberal opponent, D. C. Heron, a Catholic invited to stand by the local clergy, was an exceptionally strong candidate, representing the most congenial government formed since the union in a traditionally Liberal constituency. Yet Rossa won.

Home Rule – the first phase

Isaac Butt, originally a Tory, a distinguished lawyer, acquired considerable sympathy for Fenian men, if not for their measures, when defending Fenian prisoners in the late 1860s. He helped organise the Amnesty Association, and exploited the piqued response of some Irish conservatives to the disestablishment of the Church of Ireland by founding the Home Government Association in May 1870 to achieve a limited measure of self-government. The peeved conservative group, forming about half the founding members, soon abandoned the movement when it became clear that its success in acquiring popular support restricted their influence. If the Conservatives feared nationalist dominance of the association, Cardinal Cullen's anxiety at the danger of local Tory dominance induced him to oppose the movement. In 1868, only 37 of the 105 Irish M.P.s were Catholics, and Cullen dreaded the possibility of a Protestant Tory home rule government in Ireland. But the limits of his political power were never more starkly revealed than in 1871. Though Cullen was then apparently at the height of his political and ecclesiastical influence, fresh from the triumph of diseastablishment and of the Vatican Council, his main lay supporter, Peter Paul MacSwiney, could not find a seconder to oppose Dublin Corporation's proposed resolution in favour of home rule. Cullen's Catholic Union, established in 1872 as a rival to the Home Government Association, proved so spectacular a non-starter that it has not even prompted a Ph.D. thesis. Cullen's humiliation was complete when MacSwiney, despite clerical support, ignominiously withdrew in Meath before a home rule tenant-farmer, Nicholas Ennis, in the 1874 election. Likewise David Moriarty, the articulate episcopal meteorologist, who, though reticent about his sources, had revealed that hell was not hot enough nor eternity long enough for the Fenian leaders, found his political influence withering away in the face of the remarkable upsurge in grassroots home rule sentiment, when the electors humiliatingly returned a Protestant home ruler, Blennerhassett, against Moriarty's Catholic nominee, Dease, in the Kerry by-election of 1872. Home Rulers' success in winning nine of fourteen by-elections, mostly against Liberals supported by the higher clergy, between 1870 and 1874, indicated the degree of popular disenchantment with the Union, for no central organisation existed until November 1873, when the Home Rule League superseded the Home Government Association, which had done little more than keep local organisations informed of each other's activities. The general election in 1874 registered the most startling change in party representation since the Union. The Conservatives lost eight seats, falling from 40 to 32, the Liberals collapsed from 65 to 12, and Home Rulers won 59 seats. The rise of Home Rulers at the expense of Liberals appears far more dramatic than it proved in reality, for many sitting Liberals simply described themselves as Home Rulers to acquire popular support. Perhaps only 20 of the 59 nominal Home Rulers were genuine. Nevertheless, the very fact that Liberals felt misrepresentation necessary indicated the depth of feeling among the electorate.

Butt failed to exploit the election victory. The House of Commons contemptuously dismissed his attempts to distract its attention to Irish reforms, and began to pay attention to Irish matters only when a small group of Home Rulers, to Butt's horror, began to exploit the venerable procedures of the House to obstruct legislation on non-Irish issues by incessant talk. The obstructionists, Joseph Biggar and John O'Connor Power, both Fenians, were soon joined by Frank Hugh O'Donnell and Charles Stewart Parnell, who was returned for Meath in a by-election in 1875. They remained in a small minority within the parliamentary party, but won increasing popular support in Ireland and among the Irish in Britain, who elected Parnell to replace Butt as president of the Home Rule Confederation of Great Britain in 1877. Butt's death in May 1879 did not, however, permit Parnell achieve complete control of the party. Rather was it a conjunction of circumstances, largely arising from agricultural depression, that allowed Parnell emerge within a few years as virtual dictator of nationalist Ireland.

3   The Land War 1879–82

Economic crisis

THE agricultural crisis that began in 1877 owed something to foreign competition but much more, particularly in Connacht, to poor potato crops, which accounted for over sixty per cent of the £14 million fall in the value of Irish tillage produce between 1876 and 1879. The £3 million loss suffered on bad crops of oats likewise owed little to international competition. Protection of United Kingdom agriculture, a remedy frequently suggested in Ireland, could not have averted these disasters. The government might have acted more promptly to relieve distress, but could do little in the short term to solve a crisis different in type from the collapse in grain prices afflicting British and European agriculture. Only wheat and barley, between them responsible for a mere fifteen per cent of the total decline in the value of crops, were primarily affected by international, as distinct from domestic, influences. The crisis would have occurred even had world agricultural prices continued buoyant, for the potato failure decimated pig and poultry numbers, inflicting particularly serious losses in Mayo, where poultry numbers increased at nearly double the national rate between 1871 and 1877, and where eggs had become almost as important a source of income as pigs.

Agricultural crisis alone could not create political convulsions. The great famine had not roused Connacht to activity a generation before. As recently as 1860–62, when potato yields fell slightly below those of 1877–80 in many places, the emigration rather than the outrage statistics reflected the consequences. The American slump of 1873–79 cut off this outlet, creating in the countryside a pool of potential activists, who were left with time on their hands at home when the main supplementary source of cash income, migratory labour work, failed in 1879 due to poor British harvests. But, on past performance, the worst that these circumstances seemed to threaten was an outbreak of ribbonism, local flareups of agrarian outrage. The manner in which the tenant movement translated, for the first time in Irish history, an economic crisis for the peasantry of the west into a political problem for the government, marks a major milestone on the road to modernisation.

'The West's awake'

The genial Conservative Chief Secretary, James Lowther, 'a lively member of the Jockey Club', denied the esistence of a serious situation in Connacht, and sought instead instinctive refuge in the arcane recesses of conspiracy theory by attributing the growing unrest in 1879 to the nefarious influence of outside trouble makers. He propounded this interpretation particularly emphatically in ridiculing the Milltown land meeting to the House of Commons on 26 June 1879, 'I find, for instance, that the first resolution was moved by a clerk in a commercial house in Dublin, and seconded by a person who is stated to be a discharged schoolmaster. Another resolution moved by a convict at large upon a ticket of leave, and seconded by a person who is described as a representative of a local newspaper – and so on'. Lowther did not actually bring himself to suggest that the several thousand listeners were also Dublin clerks, rushed down to the west and dressed up as peasants to be shepherded from meeting to meeting, for he candidly conceded that 'It is, however, unfortunately the case that many tenant farmers were induced to attend the meeting and applaud the very objectionable sentiments uttered by the speakers, and thereby, no doubt, so far having involved the neighbourhood in responsibility for what occurred'. No less an authority than Frank Hugh O'Donnell, whom Michael Davitt considered as late as August 1879 the best potential leader of the land movement, later praised 'the painstaking accuracy' of Lowther's 'careful analysis' which he pronounced 'unquestionable'. How unquestionable?[5]

Apart from the fact that the first resolution at Milltown concerned the independence of Ireland, about which even Dublin clerks and discharged schoolmasters were presumably entitled to express an opinion, Lowther's dismissal of the personalities involved reveals a staggering incomprehension of developments in Connacht during the preceding five years. The early organisers of the tenant agitation formed a close-knit group, with deep western roots, who had long been involved in agrarian and political activity. The election victory of John O'Connor Power in 1874 revealed the strength of grass-roots nationalist feeling in Mayo. O'Connor Power, a Fenian initiating his own 'new departure' into constitutional politics, defeated a candidate backed by the revered archbishop of Tuam, John MacHale, the bishop of Killala and the combined priests of their dioceses.[6] O'Connor Power bore the class stigma of smallpox marks through life, having spent some of his early years in Ballinasloe workhouse. After his family emigrated to Lancashire he grew up in Rochdale, where he became a friend of Michael Davitt, and acquired considerable influence in Fenian circles in the north of England. After a short imprisonment for his part in the Fenian raid on Chester Castle he returned to study and teach in St Jarlath's College, Tuam, before entering constitutional politics. Although he remained on the Supreme Council in the IRB until 1877 many Fenians never fully forgave him for adopting constitutionalism and, regarding Power as a traitor, preferred to embrace, however cautiously, the far less radical Parnell. A fine House of Commons speaker, Power, who seemed destined for the leadership of the home rule party, failed to conceal his jealousy of Parnell, whom he dismissed as 'a mediocrity' on their first meeting, and his fierce temper and tactical mis-judgements alienated many potential allies initially attracted by his courage and confidence. The Belfast weasel, Joseph Biggar, never forgave him for being a partial rather than total obstructionist in the late 1870s, and, as Power, gnawed by frustrated ambition, became increasingly erratic in the 1880s, Parnell and Biggar hounded him out of the party. Despite his sad subsequent career, O'Connor Power played a key role in the politicisation of Mayo in the 1870s, and his election team in 1874 formed the nucleus of the subsequent tenant leadership.

His campaign manager, Matt Harris, a farmer's son who became a building contractor, was an old friend of Power's family in Ballinasloe. Matt Harris – 'I am not a man who cares very much about central bodies. My work was amongst the masses of the people' – was educated in a hedge school, and became successively O'Connellite, Young Irelander, Tenant Leaguer, Fenian and Land Leaguer. He sat as Parnellite M.P. for East Galway from 1885 until his death in 1890, played a major role in the Plan of Campaign and took the lead in opposing the Papal Rescript condemning the Plan in 1888. Harris, although the chief Fenian gunrunner in Connacht, constantly denounced divisions between constitutionalists and physical force nationalists, and formed the Ballinasloe Tenant Defence Association in 1876. His main assistants in the 1874 campaign were Thomas Brennan, Michael O'Sullivan and James Daly. Brennan, Lowther's 'com-mercial clerk from Dublin', was representative of the

North Dublin Milling Company in Castlebar in 1874, where he was in a position to acquire an intimate knowledge of local agriculture and politics. Michael O'Sullivan, Lowther's 'discharged schoolmaster', taught Matt Harris' children before being sacked from the national school on political grounds and was active from the outset in the Ballinasloe Tenant Defence Association.

James Daly, Lowther's 'representative of a local newspaper' is the most undeservedly forgotten man in Irish history. Editor of the *Connaught Telegraph,* the Castlebar newspaper which proved the land movement's most effective propaganda machine in the province, he was instrumental in focussing the attention of the national press on conditions in Mayo. Daly later quarrelled furiously with Davitt, who denounced him because 'he never had the courage to be a Fenian'. It was not the courage, but the conviction to be a Fenian that Daly, a constitutional nationalist and self-avowed conservative reformer, lacked. 'If you give facilities to create peasant proprietorship' he assured the Bessborough Commission, anticipating by a few years the collective wisdom of the Tory Party 'you would make the peasants more conservative than the Conservatives. I am a Land Leaguer myself, and I would not be a Land Leaguer if it had anything behind it like Revolutions. I would fight against it'. Few could rival Daly's detailed local knowledge. Much to the chagrin of many Fenians, who wished to boycott the enquiry, he organised the presentation of Mayo evidence which strongly influenced the Bessborough Commission to recommend radical revision of the tenurial system, and thus provided Gladstone with immediate justification for the 1881 Land Act. In only thirty per cent of the cases did landlords challenge Daly's masterly command of his material concerning exorbitant rents, in less than ten per cent did they seriously shake his evidence. William O'Brien found him in 1879 'the storm centre of the agitation . . . a rough spoken giant with an inexhaustible fund of knowledge of the people and of the quaintest mother wit', no mean tribute from such a connoisseur of quaintness as the poor man's 'People's William'! Daly hailed the arrival of representatives from the Dublin papers: 'It is the first time they ever discovered the unfortunate County Mayo on the map of Ireland. They were never done poking at the famine pits of Skibbereen, because there was a smart local doctor who wrote them up . . . two hundred thousand people died of hunger in Mayo, after living on nettles and asses flesh, and the world never said as much as "God be merciful to them".' If Daly exaggerated the incidence of famine mortality, he rightly grasped that press publicity now left no excuse for an 'information' gap. *The Daily Telegraph,* it is true, still sought, with customary perspective, to assure readers that Ireland largely escaped the September rains which deluged England – after one of the wettest Irish Septembers on record! – and that the harvest 'has not turned out badly on the whole'. But not even the credulous chief secretary could quite bring himself to believe that the clouds over Ireland poured sunshine, and the authorities came belatedly to the rescue once a flying October visit brought home to the horrified Lowther the irresponsibility of his earlier nonchalance. Relief expenditure, public and private, approached £2 million in Connacht in 1879–80, a higher rate than in 1847–8.

It was not only the emergence of a vigorous leadership cadre that distinguished the Mayo of 1878 from that of the great famine. 'Mayo – God help us' was caught in the throes of the revolution of rising expectations from the 1860s, as W. R. Larminie, an Indian civil servant, noticed on his periodic returns: 'the general rise in the scale of comfort . . . is simply enormous, and a great deal of the present distress has, I think, arisen from determination

their inability to attain Kickham's indifference to the misery surrounding them. Indeed, as early as 19 December 1877, the day of Davitt's release, Matt Harris wrote to Kickham 'pointing out the unwisdom of a certain class of nationalist, who, not satisfied with abstaining from public movements themselves, would go further and try to prevent others from doing so'. Devoy's problem was how to ensure that land agitation would not divert Fenian energies from the ultimate goal of separation, that Fenians would not become the prisoners of whatever home rulers agreed to enter into a working alliance with them to settle the land question. But which home rule leaders would cooperate with Devoy?

The Whiggish landlords and comfortable bourgeoisie who constituted the overwhelming majority of Butt's party contemplated with horror the threat of a peasant revolt. A movement of small western peasants, quite different from the respectable eastern farmers of tenant league days, seemed a throwback to ribbonism. Their organ, the *Freeman's Journal,* continued to oppose the tenant agitation until December 1879. Parnell, emerging as leader of the small advanced wing of the party, remained noncommittal in 1878 and early 1879. Although quite prepared to contemplate peasant proprietorship, Parnell was no social revolutionary, and had little desire to initiate an agrarian agitation, which would inevitably derive the bulk of its support from non-electors and might alienate the more respectable and more electorally relevant classes. The scene was transformed, however, by the startling success of the Irishtown meeting on 20 April 1879.

Though Parnell brazenly claimed a year later to have been present,[9] neither Parnell nor Devoy were involved in the Irishtown meeting. Davitt claimed credit for suggesting and organising it, but while he may have helped prepare the resolutions, it was James Daly who was the main begetter of the meeting. The account of the origins given by Daly at the meeting itself was not contradicted at the time. He had, he claimed, been approached in January by tenants from Irishtown threatened with eviction with a plea to publish details of their plight in the *Connaught Telegraph*.[10] The *Telegraph* carried an announcement of the forthcoming meeting on 15 February, a month before Davitt claims to have been approached.[11] Individual Fenians were on the platform, but overall control remained with Daly. The meeting proved an enormous success, attracting about 10,000 people, compelling national politicians and the Dublin newspapers, who initially ignored the meeting, to come to grips with this new elemental force in public life. From Parnell's viewpoint the most ominous feature was that O'Connor Power, the only M.P. to attend the meeting, stood to reap the political harvest. As it was now clear that the tenant movement had acquired a momentum of its own Parnell moved to assert his control. Devoy, Davitt and Parnell agreed on the 'new departure' at a meeting on 1 June, Parnell apparently giving vague assurances of his good intentions concerning ultimate independence in return for Devoy's promise to throw Fenian support on to his side in the land struggle. Parnell's decision to attend the Westport meeting of 8 June was no leap in the dark, but a calculated defensive decision to reassert his leadership by picking up a crown from a potato patch. It was indeed an incongruous fate which linked the destinies of the turbulent Catholic tenantry of Mayo and the apparently frigid Protestant Wicklow aristocrat, 'cold in look, cold in manner, cold in speech'.

Parnell

The rise of Parnell from the stumbling political novice of 1875 to the master politician and charismatic leader five years later constitutes the most brilliant political performance in Irish history. Intense ambition, tactical resourcefulness, superb fighting spirit – for Parnell had the courage of his ambition – and the lapses of judgement of his two main rivals, O'Connor Power and Frank Hugh O'Donnell, won him the leadership of the party. O'Connor Power, who seemed poised after Irishtown to exploit the tenant agitation, squandered his opportunity by petulantly refusing, apparently because Parnell was invited, to attend the Westport meeting. O'Donnell explained his defeat by Parnell on the grounds that the natural deference of the peasant Irish to birth inclined them instinctively towards an aristocratic leader. But it was precisely this sense of deference the Land movement was instrumental in destroying. Matt Harris did indeed placate the sensitive O'Donnell's feelings, at least according to O'Donnell, with this line of argument, but one must dismiss it as sheer kindness. For it was the same Matt Harris who asserted after the Irishtown meeting that 'my reliance is in the people – in the people alone – to others the co-operation of the gentry may seem a great advantage, but for my part I regard it as our greatest danger,[12] and again at Westport 'hitherto the masses could not hold a meeting without having his Honour of the big house, or, at least, some shoneen of a J.P. to preside over them. All that is now changed'.[13] O'Donnell's concept of leadership consisted of asserting that because he was cleverer than everybody else they should automatically defer to him. He denounced the self-educated Davitt and Devoy because 'it seems never to have occurred to either of them that they owed any deference or obedience to the educated, responsible opinion of Ireland' – i.e. to Frank Hugh O'Donnell, graduate of Queen's College Galway. One hardly needs to resort to theories concerning the peasant Irish concept of aristocratic leadership to explain the failure of someone who believes that examination results constitute a criterion of political capacity to struggle to the top of the greasy pole. Had Parnell been the graduate of Queen's College Galway and O'Donnell the Wicklow aristocrat, who can envisage Frank Hugh – appropriately nicknamed Crank Hugh – eating Parnell's heart? Davitt likewise explained his failure to attain national leadership on the grounds that he was a mere peasant, while Parnell was a landlord. The simple fact was that Parnell possessed political talents that O'Connor Power, O'Donnell and Davitt conspicuously lacked. True, all three might plead the inexperience of youth for their tactical errors. O'Connor Power and Davitt were thirty-three in 1879, O'Donnell thirty-one. But Parnell himself was only thirty-three. He was ten years younger than Joseph Chamberlain, thirteen years younger than Charles Dilke, the coming men of the Liberal party. There have been younger physical force leaders in Irish history, though only Collins achieved comparable stature, but whereas youth enjoys natural advantages in the game of the gun, Parnell's political performance, after only four years experience of parliament, has never been matched in Irish politics. It took both O'Connell and de Valera 15 years longer to acquire a similar sureness of touch.

Parnell's anti-English feelings, if such they were, are frequently attributed to the influence of his American mother, but Davitt, who had little reason to exonerate him, considered him merely contemptuous of the organised hypocrisy of parliament towards Ireland, not of the English as a people. He certainly despised the Irish at least as much as the English, but the supercilious Saxon air keenly rankled the Anglo-Irish aristocrat. 'The instinct of snobbery' which, as Parnell perceptively put it, 'rather seems to compel some Irishmen to worship at the shrine of English prejudice, and to bow down before the voice and censure of the English press will never gain anything for Ireland, and will only secure for such panderers the secret contempt of English-men'. Calculation thus reinforced inclination. Many were to hate Parnell, but none could despise him. He probably owes more of his temperament than of his specific phobias to his mother, who seems to have found difficulty in communicating love to her children. Most of the Parnell children were extremely lonely, which may help explain the influence of the mother figure, Mrs O'Shea, a thirteenth child, in whose respect Parnell conquered his intense superstition.

Parnell's genius lay less in conceptual originality or in the incisiveness of his social analysis than in the sensitivity of his political antennae, in grasping the minimum that would arouse and unite the country, and the maximum concession that could be extracted from the government. Finally convinced by the success of the Irishtown meeting that the land question would be the engine which would draw home rule in its train, the crucial question henceforth was who would the engine driver be? Less important, but far from irrelevant, who would the passengers be? How many first class? Parnell hesitated about peasant proprietorship partly because he feared that Westminster might feel less disposed to grant home rule to a people who had emasculated the political power of the aristocracy.

Parnell gave a masterly performance at Westport. After laconically dismissing Archbishop MacHale's warning not to attend the meeting, on the grounds that he was sure the archbishop would not wish him to break his word to the organisers, he ridiculed the Fenian fear that government concessions would sap the national fibre, preached conciliation with the landlords while simultaneously urging the tenants 'keep a firm hold on your homesteads and lands'. In contrast to the customary lachrymose invocations to God's love for his persecuted children, Parnell confined his speculations on divine intentions to applied theology. His sole reference to the Deity was to remind his listeners that 'God helps him who helps himself'.

For the rest of 1879 Parnell acted primarily as a restraining influence on Davitt, whose position was more ambiguous, simply because, although a distinctly more devious character than he has customarily been given credit for, he, unlike Parnell or even Devoy, did genuinely care about the plight of the peasantry. During the summer he wrested local initiative from James Daly, forestalling Daly's plan to establish a Tenants Defence Association of Mayo by founding the Land League of Mayo on 16 August 1879. J. J. Louden, a Westport barrister who had borne the expenses of the June meeting, became president and Daly vice-president, reversing their positions in the Castlebar Tenants' Defence Association established ten months previously. But when Davitt proceeded to organise a national land league Parnell decisively intervened in October to dilute the radical reform message 'the Land for the People' contained in the preamble of the Land League of Mayo into the more specific terms of 'rent reductions' calculated to appeal to a moderate reform body in the country at large. After the Westport meeting he didn't return to Connacht until November, when 'with a falcon's eye for his chance' he swooped on Balla to prevent a series of scheduled evictions, winning spectacular publicity that concealed the essential moderation of his policy behind a romantic fighting façade. His tour of America with Davitt and John Dillon in the spring of 1880 raised urgently needed money and asserted his ascendancy in John Devoy's own bailiwick. He was fortunate too that the recovery of the American economy enabled Irish Americans to place far more money at his disposal, £250,000 between 1879 and 1882, than would otherwise have been the case. The American tour was a triumph, in terms of publicity, money and power.

Popular support for Parnell far outran his strength among the electors, as recorded in the general election of April 1880. The real issue was whether the Whig wing under William Shaw, or the New Departure wing under Parnell would gain control of the party. The struggle revolved around the attitude to the Land League, and the fact that a remarkable group of young men entered parliament for the first time on a Parnellite ticket should not divert attention from the strength of the resistance under Shaw, which places Parnell's insistence on moderation in realistic parliamentary perspective. Although elected chairman of the party in May, Parnell could count on only twenty-four loyal supporters compared with Shaw's twenty-one, while fourteen members waited to back the winner.

Agitation

The initial agitation in 1879 among the Connacht tenants cannot be attributed primarily to outside agitators lacking local connections. This does not dispose however, of the argument employed by W. E. Forster, Lowther's successor as Chief Secretary when the Liberals returned to power after the 1880 general election, by Gladstone himself, and by the Special Commission on Parnell and Crime in 1888. All three attributed the marked increase in outrage after the good harvest of 1880, despite declining evictions, to the influence of Davitt and Parnell, as expressed, for instance, in Parnell's support for boycotting in his Ennis speech in September.

The first crucial feature of the winter of 1880 was that, although the national potato crop recovered from the trough of 1879, yields in Mayo and Galway fell thirty-five per cent below the national average. In these areas 'the good harvest' of government spokesmen was a figment of the official imagination. Anxiety increased in Mayo as incipient signs of blight were detected once more in July,[14] and as a cholera epidemic, widespread by the summer, helped reduce the number of poultry by seventeen per cent during 1880, compared with the national decline of only three per cent. The rejection by the Tory House of Lords of the Compensation for Disturbance Bill, proposing higher compensation for eviction, on 4 August – historic anniversary – just as the potato failed for the fourth season in a row, strengthened the will to resist the threat of eviction which now hung over half the holdings of Connacht.

While the conspiracy thesis carries as little conviction in the case of Connacht in 1880 as in 1879, it seems at first sight more plausible in the case of Kerry, the other major centre of disturbance. The Special Commissioners pointed out that only 5 agrarian crimes were recorded in 1878, 13 in 1879, but 298 in 1880, of which only 69 occurred in the first nine months, compared with 229 after the organisation of the Land League in October. As distress had been more acute earlier in the year, the Commissioners considered the increase in outrage inexplicable except as a consequence of conspiracy. Although the Commissioners mode of argument diverts attention from the fact that 69 outrages in the first nine months represented a striking increase over 1879, it is certainly true that a further marked intensification occurred in the final three months, until by the end of 1880 Kerry jostled with Mayo and Galway at the top of the outrage league table.

The economic structure of north and central Kerry, the most disturbed parts of the county, presents a clear contrast to that of Mayo. The Kerry tenants were far more prosperous, farming on average, 50 acres of good land compared with 15 acres of poor land in Mayo. The potato yield in Kerry fell only slightly below the national yield in 1880. If any area seems ripe for the conspiracy interpretation it is north Kerry. Nevertheless a combination of local and, in contrast to Connacht, international

The Land War: places mentioned in the text

factors provide an obvious explanation for the growth of outrage in such apparently unpropitious circumstances.

Kerry, like Mayo, underwent an exceptionally rapid silent social revolution in the 1870s. Illiteracy, having fallen from seventy to forty-seven per cent between 1841 and 1871, fell to thirty-five per cent by 1881. Pre-famine marriage patterns persisted even more tenaciously until the 1870s in Kerry than elsewhere in the west, and the disruptive impact of the demographic changes tradition-ally associated with post-famine Ireland were con-centrated into a particularly short and traumatic period. Age at marriage increased more rapidly than in any other county during the 1870s. In 1871, thirty-four per cent of females aged 20–24 were married, in 1881 only twenty-one per cent. Over the same period the number of unmarried males aged 20–29 rose twenty-seven per cent in Kerry compared with seven per cent in Munster. In the Listowel poor law union a thirty per cent increase in the number of single men, and a decline of forty per cent in the number of married men, in this age group, reflected the abrupt reduction in marriage and inheritance opportunities. Nevertheless, Kerry actually experienced a two per cent increase in population between 1871 and 1881, for the emigration escape route to America was dammed up at precisely the period when marital pat-terns were changing with unprecedented rapidity, leaving a potentially large number of potential recruits for agitation in the active age group.

This primarily dairying area prospered with the boom-ing butter and pork prices of the 1870s–butter at £7 a cwt 'eight months all round' in 1876–and suffered especially seriously from the fifty per cent fall in butter prices in 1879–80. Cow numbers fell by only the national average, about nine per cent, between 1877 and 1881, but this had exceptionally severe repercussions in an area with double the national cow density and in a sector where numbers rarely fluctuated to this extent – the fall between 1879 and 1880 was the highest recorded between 1863 and 1925. The dairying crisis, accentuated by the potato failure of 1879, affected pig numbers, which fell by thirty per cent from 1879 and 1880 compared with the twenty per cent national decline, and recovered much more slowly than the national rate in 1881. The contrasts in the type of agriculture help explain why Kerry lagged 18 months behind Mayo in the agitation calendar.

Some rent increases in the mid 1870s, tolerable in boom circumstances, ensured that the ensuing slump would be all the more severely felt, and the vigorous activity of land agents, especially S. M. Hussey, supplied the spark for the timber. Hussey was already deeply unpopular before 1880. He incurred much ill-will by outbidding his tenants for the Harenc Estate, which they had hoped to purchase under the provisions of the Bright Clause (for the encouragement of peasant proprietorship) in the 1870 Land Act and for which Hussey bid, as he candidly conceded, as a pure speculation. Unrest began to spread as evictions rose so rapidly that Kerry had the highest eviction rate in the country for the first nine months of 1880. Evictions in both the second and third quarters of 1880 exceeded the total number for 1879. The first outrage near Castleisland, henceforth a hotbed of agitation, occurred on 10 September, when a party of armed men reinstated on her holding the evicted Widow Leary. Hussey retorted by burning the houses of future evictees to prevent reinstatement. This policy provoked moves to establish the Land League in Kerry. The first branch was founded in Tralee on 25 September, a second was established in Castleisland a few days later following the eviction of Patrick Murphy of Rath. Murphy offered no resistance to the actual eviction of his family of eleven, but lost his self-control when the house 'which had been floored and ceiled by Murphy a short time before was burned in their sight'. The Land League's policy of fighting fire with fire eventually made life rather too hot for Hussey, who fled the country in 1884 after being himself burned out. The final impetus to intense agitation in Kerry came from the outstanding local leadership of the editor of the *Kerry Sentinel,* Tim Harrington, who subsequently proved one of the ablest national organisers in the Parnellite party.

Gladstone's immediate response to the accelerating tempo of terror in late 1880 was to introduce stringent coercion, empowering the authorities to imprison any 'reasonably suspected' person under two Acts passed in February and March 1881. The coercion debates provide revealing indications of the comprehension gap which prevented the official mind from understanding the natives. Forster's impressive familiarity with details of local outrages testified to intensive study of the crime statistics. He refrained from examining the local agricultural returns, apparently labouring under the impression that *local* crime reports should be correlated with *national* agricultural statistics. He thus not only failed to relate outrage to local economic factors, but also misunderstood the relationship between Land League meetings and agrarian crime, on which he based the demand for coercion. At the national level, meetings and outrages increased in 1880. But at the local level no close correlation existed. Only fifteen per cent of meetings were held in Mayo, west Galway and Kerry, which together accounted for forty-five per cent of the outrages. Between September and December 1880, 13 meetings and 24 outrages were recorded in Kilkenny: 16 meetings, 247 outrages in Kerry. Forster shirked the research which would explain why Kerrymen were more inherently 'evil' than Kilkennymen. The failure of the Coercion Acts – 955 local leaders were imprisoned under their provisions, but outrages increased from 2,500 in 1880 to

4,400 in 1881 – belied Forster's fond belief that coercion would seriously diminish agrarian crime, and suitably rewarded the general intellectual poverty of his analysis.

The advantages of hindsight did not suffice to enable the special commission of 1888 to guard against the erroneous assumption which marred Forster's judgement. The Commission consisted merely of three Tory Judges – honourable men, but quite unqualified to evaluate evidence concerning a sociologically faraway society of which they knew little. They faithfully repeated Forster's analytical errors, dwelling in detail on local crime statistics, resolutely ignoring the relevant agricultural returns. They too simply assumed that Mayo gorged itself on a bountiful harvest in 1880. Even within their special province of crime their own evidence hardly sustains the argument based on it. They conclude that 'the increase in evictions which began in 1879 . . . was the result of the agitation against the Landlords': but their own supporting table records a doubling of evictions from 463 in 1877 to 980 in 1878, the highest number since 1864, before rising to 1,238 in 1879, suggesting that the agitation developed as a response to increasing evictions rather than vice versa.[15]

Concession

Parnell and his followers were ejected from the House of Commons in February 1881 for protesting vociferously at Davitt's arrest under the new coercion legislation. Compelled to choose between continuing as a parliamentary leader, or retreating to Ireland and relying exclusively on agitation, Parnell choose to continue his constitutional tactics. Despite excited private dissent by a minority, he had little difficulty in rallying the country behind him, for coercion proved merely the prelude to a major Land Act which effectively conceded the three Fs – fair rent, fixity of tenure, and free sale. To mollify his extreme wing Parnell feigned dissatisfaction with the

Act, and on 16 September he persuaded the Land League Convention to 'test the Act' in the public assurance that trial cases would expose the hollowness of the Act, but in the private conviction that 'it does not abolish land-lordism, but it will make landlordism intolerable for the landlords'. In denouncing the Act, Parnell deliberately used such provocative language – partly because he feared that the Land League, running out of funds to support evicted tenants, might lose its momentum during the winter – that he was imprisoned in Kilmainham in October. Prodded by several colleagues he issued the No-Rent Manifesto from jail on 18 October, directing the tenants to institute a rent strike. The Land League was immediately suppressed, and the Manifesto, as Parnell anticipated, failed miserably, for the Land Act, in practice, divided the tenants into two groups. As the land courts established under the Act to arbitrate fair rents immediately began reducing average rentals by nearly twenty per cent, eligible tenants naturally flocked into the courts to take advantage of this unprecedented con-cession. But the tenants most urgently in need of relief, those still in arrears of rent – one-third of tenants through-out the country, nearly two-thirds in Mayo – as well as lease holders, were ineligible for reductions. This naturally whetted the indignation of those excluded, and although Parnell had prophesied that Captain Moonlight would take his place, he underrated the depth of support on which the Captain could draw. Anna Parnell founded the Ladies Land League to maintain morale during the imprisonment of the leaders, but the real crunch came, as in earlier phases, from grassroots initiative. The vigour of local response – 3,498 outrages were recorded between October 1881 and April 1882 compared with 2,633 between October 1880 and April 1881 – convinced Gladstone and Parnell that an arrangement had to be found. Parnell had no intention of vacating the engine driver's seat for anyone. The Kilmainham Treaty, under which he was released on 2 May 1882, represented his reaction to the threat posed by the success of Captain Moonlight. The Treaty was an extraordinarily good bargain for him. He made no specific concessions to Gladstone, merely giving meaningless promises to discourage agitation and generally support Liberal measures. In return he received specific assurances that coercion would be dropped and the arrears of rent wiped out so that the ineligible tenants could take advantage of the Land Act.

The Phoenix Park murders, when Lord Frederick Cavendish, just arrived in Ireland to implement the new conciliatory policy, and T. H. Burke, the long serving under-secretary in Dublin Castle, were murdered on 6 May by members of a secret society, the Invincibles, helped obscure the significance of the Kilmainham Treaty. The murders forced nationalist ranks to rally around Parnell, widely denounced by Unionists as the instigator of the crime, and distracted attention from the policy issues involved in the Treaty. Even had the murders not occurred, however, it seems highly unlikely that proponents of continuing agitation could have effectively challenged a Parnell reinforced by the promise of the Arrears Act, which removed the main grievance on which the masses could be mobilised. The Special Commissioners on Parnell and Crime, did, it is true, indulge their obsession with conspiracy to the extent of attributing the decline in outrage to the Crimes Act of July rather than to the Arrears Act, heralded in April and introduced on 15 May, on the grounds that as the Land Act of 1881 led to no decline in crime there seemed no reason why the Arrears Act should. This ignored the fact that three-fifths of Connacht farmers did not qualify for rent reductions under the Land Act, whereas they almost all benefited from the Arrears Act. In their endeavour to emphasise the fall in outrages from 231 in July to 85 in December 1882, the Commissioners ignore their own evidence, which records a decline from the peak of 542 in March to 231 in July, before the Crimes Act came into operation but after the Arrears Bill had been promised.[16] The Crimes Act did not reverse a trend, but, at most, slightly accentuated it.

Parnell has sometimes been criticised for diverting the social revolutionary train into the safe siding of home rule in the Kilmainham Treaty. This is a misreading of the situation. The only social revolutionary policy that commanded widespread support in the country was peasant proprietorship, and the Arrears Act, by increasing security of tenure, took a significant step in that direction. The Arrears Act was the small farmers' charter. The state paid £800,000 rent for 130,000 tenants, who were now too intent on scampering to the land courts to resort to frequent outrage. The improved harvest of 1881 did nothing to banish the threat of eviction haunting the farmers of Connacht, but while the 1882 potato yield fell below that of 1881, the cancellation of arrears and average rent reductions of about twenty per cent sufficed to defuse a still potentially explosive situtation and to bring the grassroots firmly under Parnellite control. The only other social revolutionary policy that could draw on mass support, mainly in the west, was the distribution of grazing lands among existing small holders and landless men, as originally proposed by O'Connor Power, Matt Harris and James Daly. But this did not imply support for land nationalisation, as Michael Davitt found when Harris and Daly, their ears close to the Connacht ground, savagely denounced his nationalisation scheme in June 1882.[17] The man in the field decisively rejected land nationalisation. Davitt's politically fatuous proposal diverted attention from the more realistic redistribution programme, which might have dramatically altered the pattern of land holding, and condemned himself to a career of relative ineffectuality.

4   The Significance of the Land War

Deference

The Arrears Act sapped the vitality of the most remarkable mass movement in Irish history. In composition,
tactics and ideology, the Land League ranked among the
most effective and sophisticated movements of rural
agitation in nineteenth-century Europe. The curb placed
on the power of 13,000 landlords, 800 of whom owned
half the country, over 400,000 tenants – 100,000 lease-
holders remained excluded from the 1881 Act until
1887 – did not, of course, create equality of opportunity
in the countryside, but it greatly reduced the most glaring
existing inequality, and gave a powerful stimulus to the
struggle to emancipate tenants from the shackles of
mental serfdom. The Land League taught the tenants
the simple but symbolic gesture of not doffing their caps
to landlords. The tenants themselves adopted the equally
simple if somewhat less symbolic technique of increasingly directing their assaults against landlords and their
representatives, hitherto largely immune from physical
disincentive. From 1844 to 1878 bailiffs and process
observers suffered less than one per cent of agrarian
'offences against the person', in 1879 twelve per cent and
in 1880 twenty per cent. The age of deference in rural
Ireland was coming to an end with a bang when nearly
half the total assaults in Mayo in the final quarter of 1880
were perpetrated directly on landlords or their represen-

tatives. The largest proportionate increase in the type of agrarian offence recorded between 1877 and 1881 was 'taking and holding forcible possession', i.e. returning to one's holding after eviction, repudiating the state as a landlord agent by refusing to defer to the legitimacy of the law in the person of the bailiff.

The contemptuous reaction to the denunciation of the Ladies Land League by Archbishop McCabe of Dublin, pointed to another area where the sense of deference waned as lay power waxed. McCabe was actually threatened with assassination in 1880 on account of his hostility to the Land League. The Church initially glanced askance at the land movement. Whereas two priests launched the Callan tenant league in 1849, no priests were involved in the original organisation of the Mayo tenant movement. Not until the Claremorris meeting of 13 July 1879, after the Irishtown, Westport and Milltown meetings had generated an irresistible momentum, did a priest appear on a tenant platform,[18] a far cry from the days when O'Connell's Catholic association would have foundered without clerical participation. Nearly fifty per cent of the delegates to Gavan Duffy's tenant league convention in 1850 were priests, compared with only four per cent at the first Land League Convention. Nevertheless, the extent to which clerical influence was curbed should not be exaggerated by isolating incidents like the refusal to allow Canon Ulick Burke to include resolutions about the temporal power of the papacy and the education question at Land League meetings in Mayo, or Bishop Gillooly's failure to establish a clerically dominated league in Roscommon, or the refusal of the parishioners of Skreen to accept a new priest when the bishop of Killala removed a pro-Land League cleric in 1881. For the clergy, whether reasoning like Bishop McEvilly of Galway, who believed that 'the people require to be treated, at present, like children' and that 'whether the priests will it or no the meetings will be held . . . if the priests attend they will keep the people attached to them', or out of simple conviction about the justice of the cause, were alert enough to align themselves gradually with the new movement. Priests sprung from tenant stock naturally shared many of the attitudes of their parishioners, though not all displayed such indifference to technical niceties as Fr Thomas Higgins, a Loughrea curate, when threatening anyone who broke the national oath in 1881 that he 'would put a rope round his neck and hang him; he should be shot . . .'.[19] No Fenian could fault the diagnosis of Fr O'Malley of the Neale who coined the term boycotting when his parishioners couldn't wrap their tongues round 'ostracisation'. O'Malley eulogised the clergy of the once established Church – 'after all the Protestant clergyman lived amongst the people, spent his money amongst the people, was a kindly and good neighbour to the people' – the better to set up the landlords for the polemical kill: 'what is the object of the Land League? It is to do away once and for-ever with the curse of Ireland – Irish landlordism (groans for it). What is Irish landlordism in this country? It is the garrison of the enemy . . .'. Where the clergy responded to popular feelings they took their customary place in the vanguard of the movement; where they failed to respond, they were simply ignored, like Archdeacon O'Connell, whose opposition to the Land League did not long post-pone Castleisland's emergence as a main centre of agitation.[20] The land courts established by the Land League withdrew from priests much of their authority as arbitrators of land disputes, a field in which they had generally played an active mediating role. Deference in ecclesiastical matters of course continued, but the role of the priest in society became increasingly circumscribed as major areas of social life were transferred from his informal jurisdiction to specialised agencies.

The lay leadership itself was the servant rather than the master of the movement. Leaders like Davitt, Brennan and Egan, however prominent initially, found their influence eroded once they defied the popular will. The farmers' rejection of the No-Rent Manifesto, signed, however cynically, by Parnell himself, clearly illustrated the limits of the leaders' power. Davitt blamed Ulster tenants for frustrating the League's policy of testing the land act by rushing into the land courts, but although the highest absolute number of applicants for relief came from Ulster, the highest proportionate number of those eligible came from his own beloved Connacht.

In this respect the political significance of the decline of the agricultural labourers since the famine became particularly relevant. Tension between labourers and farmers was widespread before the famine, and rural class relations would presumably have been far more strained in 1880 had the proportion of labourers to farmers remained at its pre-famine level. Despite the dwindling proportion of labourers, class hostility still occasionally erupted in the post-famine countryside. Anxious though James Stephens was to improve the labourers' lot, he played down the land issue for fear of alienating farmers from Fenianism. Where agricultural labourers still comprised a high proportion of the rural population, as in the Kanturk area of Co. Cork, frightened farmers and landlords felt sufficiently menaced by incipient labourers' movements to grant wage increases during the 1870s. Threatening rumbles from labourers induced the Land League to change its title to the Land League and Labourers and Industrial Movement in 1880 and, more concretely, to support legislation for improving labourers' housing conditions. Three thousand labourers' cottages were sanctioned between 1882 and 1892 by local authorities in Cork, much the largest number in any county. It was particularly fortunate for the League that the proportion of labourers in Connacht, where small farmers predominated, was exceptionally low.

The land agitation achieved the largest active mass participation of any movement in Irish history, mobilising sectors of the population and areas of the country just beginning to become politicised. It raised newspaper circulation to unprecedented levels, harnessing the mass popular support for the land campaign. *United Ireland*, founded by Parnell and edited by William O'Brien occasionally sold 100,000 copies, dwarfing the circulation of any previous Irish newspaper – the *Nation* sold 10,000 copies at the height of its fame forty years earlier. In addition, Patrick Ford's *Irish World* touched a weekly circulation of 20,000 in Ireland during 1880. The Ballinahinch priest who asserted in 1881 that the Land League 'has made the farmers a reading people, and men who some time ago would be ashamed to speak before half a dozen people can now come to this platform and make able speeches'[21] exaggerated the speed, but not the direction, of rural change. The Special Commission on Parnell and Crime failed to make any allowance for the modernisation of rural mentalities when arguing that only conspiracy could have caused more agrarian crimes (4,439) in 1881, when only 3,465 families were evicted, than in the four years 1849–53, when 58,423 families were evicted.[22] The implication that what was good enough for the fathers should be good enough for the sons failed to take account of the transformation wrought in the meantime, for the Land League generation travelled further in historical time than all previous generations in Irish history.

The Ladies Land League, inspired by American models, represented an unprecedented initiative in female participation in public life. Female involvement in the struggle for the land was common throughout the nineteenth century. Process servers in execution of their duty not infrequently failed to salvage their dignity from hordes of howling women. But the formal organisation of female protest was unheard of. Some clerics, in Ireland and America, usually more familiar with urban parlours than with rural kitchens, felt their masculinity so outraged at the mere thought of a ladies land league that they considered themselves compelled to denounce the perils to feminine modesty of this departure from the demure ways of Victorian damseldom. Clerical denunciation proved ineffective and Anna Parnell became the first woman to feature in an active rather than passive role in modern Irish public affairs. Female support proved indispensable for the success of boycotting, heavily dependent on the housewife avoiding prescribed shops. The institutionalisation of the boycotting technique, which demanded remarkable self discipline and total communal participation fostered a widespread sense of personal involvement in the struggle. As the *Annual Register* revealingly observed 'reasoning from the ordinary notions of race, the most celtic of celtic peoples and therefore the most subject to blind mysteries and the most incapable of steady combinations could have hardly been expected to give effect to advice which demanded for its fulfilment wide organisation and rigid discipline'.[23]

Consciousness

Had the Land League merely succeeded in effectively articulating the long suppressed aspirations of the peasantry, that, in itself, would have constituted a considerable political achievement. But the League did more. It pioneered on a mass basis a technique destined to become indispensable in nationalist agitation, the appeal to spurious historic rights. Celtic Ireland had been an intensely hierarchical society, the bulk of the people possessing only a tenuous and ill-defined share in the property for which the leading families contended. The information available to late nineteenth-century commentators did suggest that something like genuine communal property rights may have existed, and Michael Davitt devoted his preamble to the constitution of the Land League of Mayo to an exposition of the historic rights of cultivators in Celtic Ireland. But if the modernisation of tenurial systems was to be wrapped in the swaddling clothes of historical reincarnation, Davitt soon found himself outmanoeuvred by more astute historiographical tacticians, and 'the land for the people' acquired the distinctly contemporary connotation of individual instead of communal proprietorship.

Perhaps the most striking feature of Land League propaganda was the success with which it subsumed local under national grievances. Local details were now used to illuminate national themes and local piecemeal social engineering ceased to exercise much attraction as a solution to peasant problems. Consciousness, in the familiar modern manner, came to focus increasingly on impersonal rather than personal obstacles, on the institution of landlordism itself rather than on individual landlords. Few tenants, except those descended from genuinely dispossessed native landowners, challenged the legitimacy of landlordism before the famine. The behaviour of many landlords during the famine, and the facility with which property rights were acquired under the Encumbered Estates Act led to a distinction being drawn between 'good' and 'bad' landlords. In the immediate wake of the famine, moderate nationalist observers described 'good landlords' as 'the real bona fida landowners of the soil'. Popular commentators acknowledged that 'a good landlord has inevitably a good body of tenants. Both are bound together by mutuality and gratitude . . . long may they continue so![24] They exploited the opportunity less to condemn landlordism than merely to equate 'good' with Gaelic, contrasting the generous behaviour of the remnants of 'the humane old aristocracy of Ireland' with that of the descendants of 'Cromwell's drummers, Highland Pipers or Saxon pantry boys'.[25] Thirty years later James Daly still conceded the rights of 'good' landlords to their property, but to him 'a good landlord was as rare as a white blackbird'. In so far as the Mayo farmers of 1879 had any recollection of a native system of land tenure, it was rundale, which the famine obliterated and to which they showed little disposition to return. That their sons should aspire to be their own masters, to consider themselves the legitimate owners of their holdings, constituted a revolution in mentalities which the deferential famine generation could scarcely credit. Davitt's story of the old Mayo man listening to a speaker advocating 'a complete abolition of landlords' asking 'Arrah, to who do we pay the rint, thin, Sir?'[26] hardly suggests a deeply rooted conviction in the peasant breast of an inalienable immemorial right to the land. The despoiled historic rights to which the tillers of the soil laid claim were conjured from the imagination of the living generation. The peasant mind showed little of its fabled conservatism when it grasped the implications of the new historic rights, a realisation which reflected the promptings not of a timeless voice from the grave but of astute propagandists from the platform. In 1881 the bulk of the people were still satisfied with rent reductions and relative security of tenure, their original aims, though no longer as the ultimate goal but merely as a step on the road to peasant proprietorship. The Land League not merely articulated, but largely created, that aspiration, legitimised it with an immaculate pedigree by which the tenants acquired retrospective private shares in a mythical Gaelic garden of Eden, and pushed it through to within sight of ultimate victory. It was a virtuoso performance.

The absence of a strong populist or peasantist streak distinguishes Land League ideology from that of most European rural movements. The League was not at all anti-urban. It confined criticisms of the town to predatory urban landlords, and rarely indulged in glorification of arcadian virtues. O'Connor Power, Daly and Harris advocated large scale reclamation, taxes on absentees and improved housing for tenants, but they fostered few fond *narodnik* illusions about the intrinsic virtues of rural life. Far from idealising 'the noble peasant' Harris suspected 'that when the farmers would be emancipated and get their land, such men would look on the boundary of their farms as the boundary of their country, because farmers as a rule are very selfish men'.[27] Harris conceded that the Government 'disestablished the Protestant church' but 'they also disestablished our manufactures, trade and commerce'.[28] Daly considered 1881 memorable not only for the Land Act but for the stimulus allegedly given to national manufactures by the Dublin Exhibition.[29] *United Ireland* defined from the outset industrialisation as a goal, devoting the first column of its first issue to pleas from Parnell, Archbishop Croke and the Lord Mayor of Dublin to foster Irish industry. It concentrated more attention on industrialisation than any other national paper, considering a prosperous agriculture not an alternative to, but the basis of, manufacturing development. It was not Land League, but landlord spokesmen who romanticised pre-industrial society. When Lord Clanrickarde's agent lamented the alleged idleness of women consequent on the decline of domestic weaving and spinning he was curtly reminded that shop goods were cheaper.

The tension between town and country, which many historians detect on the continent, barely existed in Ireland. Irish towns were overwhelmingly rural, their economies becoming intimately linked with the surrounding countryside as agriculture became evermore intensively commercialised. Castlebar, for instance, had a population of 3,900 in 1881. The five largest occupational categories among adult males were soldier (there was a barracks in the town), general labourer (many of whom were agricultural labourers), shoemaker or dealer, agricultural labourer and farmer. More specifically urban occupations lagged well behind. Towns reflected the relative prosperity of the countryside rather than vice versa. It was not because urban Connacht but became rural Connacht was retarded in 1850 that the Tenant League failed to flourish in the province. It was because rural rather than urban Connacht changed so markedly in the following thirty years that the land movement struck such deep roots in 1879. Urban commercial people depended for their income on the prosperity of the farmer; were intimately involved in his credit transactions; were themselves frequently first generation migrants from agriculture, relatives of local farmers or even farmers themselves. 'Merchants' like Thomas O'Rourke, secretary of the Land League in Tralee and earlier a central figure in the Kerry Tenants' Defence Association, who had 'a large acquaintance with the farmers of the country for a number of years', 'provision merchants' like Joseph Biggar, 'cattle dealers and butchers' like P. J. Condon M.P., mayor of Clonmel in 1888 and Bernard Colleary, M.P., mayor of Sligo in 1891, 'merchants and farmers' like John Connolly, mayor of Sligo in 1888, 'town commissioners and tenant farmers' like John O'Hagan, chairman of the Carrickmacross town council; and 'publicans, hotel keepers and farmers' like M. Murphy, proprietor of the Crown Hotel at Castleisland, and W. H. O'Sullivan, triumphant Home Rule candidate in Co. Limerick in 1874 and subsequently a secretary of the Land League, were businessmen who had naturally a close grasp of agricultural reality. An urban address in Ireland by no means implied as blissful an innocence of agriculture as it frequently did in England. Several professional men concealed farming experience behind urban occupational nomenclature, thus misleading urban historians into emphasising their lack of contact with agriculture. J. J. Louden held seven thousand acres. James Daly farmed extensively; 'I pay rent to four landlords. I am a newspaper proprietor by accident: farming is my forte'.[30] Ireland cannot be imprisoned in the urban historians' synthetic straitjacket of 'town versus country'.

Economic consequences

Despite its remarkable political and psychological achievements, the triumph of the Land League contained ominous implications for the formulation of policy in an independent Ireland. The land legislation concealed within itself the seeds, if not of disaster, then of disillusion. For while the Land Act was essentially a victory for social and political ideals, the tenant case relied largely on economic arguments, in the belief that the magic of property would turn sand into gold, that once a tenant became his own master, once protected from the disincentive effects of a constantly spiralling rent, he would cultivate his holding incomparably more efficiently than hitherto. This belief rested more on acts of faith and hope than on an incisive analysis of Irish agriculture. For it no more occurred to Land League leaders than to government officials to actually study the evidence to assess the probable economic consequences of tenurial reform. They seemed to share the attitude of an arch enemy, S. M. Hussey, who passionately protested against the burden of knowledge 'when a man thinks of the vast amount of information buried beyond all probable excavation in the Blue Books of the last fifty years, he may well break into Carlyle – like diatribes against the waste of the whole thing – which is paid for out of the taxpaper's pocket'. Land League leaders allowed their economic analysis to be no more incommoded than Hussey's rollicking recollections by Blue Book, or any other, facts.

The early Connacht leaders drew heavily on the precedents of France, Belgium and Prussia, whose agriculture they believed to have flourished through the introduction of peasant proprietorship or, more radically, through the redistribution of the largest farms among small holders. The argument from continental analogy was not supported by reliable information, and these tenant leaders recreated modern European agrarian history almost as imaginatively as ancient Irish history. But however crude their use of evidence, the early demands of O'Connor Power, Harris and Daly for the redistribution of the graziers land[31] – as late as 1911 the 6,000 largest farmers in Connacht held roughly the same amount of land as the 70,000 smallest holders – attempted to grapple with the fact that many existing holdings were simply too small to support a family even if rent were abolished. Parnell and the propertied elements he attracted to the Land League drew a discreet veil over this potentially disruptive demand, concentrating on the more politically realistic and socially conservative goal of turning tenants into proprietors on their existing holdings, however miserable.

These leaders were as ready as Unionists to portray the Irish tenant as a feckless fellow, though hastening to excuse his fecklessness on grounds of extortionate rents. This approach caricatured the farmer's attitude towards money. The alacrity and alertness with which the farmer responded to market stimulae, not only after the Land Acts, but equally emphatically before them, belies the belief that fear of increased rents rendered him indifferent to economic incentive. The rational rural response to price movements demolishes the argument that excessive rents prevented accumulation of capital. Rents, averaging about £13 million per annum, probably accounted for a somewhat lower proportion, twenty to twenty-five per cent, of the value of agricultural output than in England. The farmer's ground for complaint, apart from the fact that the peculiar English tenurial system should be imposed on Ireland in the first place, lay less in the level of rent than in the arbitrariness with which it might be altered, and in the tragic increase of evictions. These entailed not only loss of job but destruction of social status, when arrears began to accumulate, as they inevitably did after a run of bad harvests – not normally after one bad year, but after two or three successive failures, as between 1860–62 and again between 1877–80. In this respect the number of recorded evictions, never reaching 0·5 per cent per annum after 1852, provides a quite inadequate index of the insecurity of the tenants' situation. Ejection notices greatly exceeded the number of evictions, and in 1862 and 1881 the threat of eviction hovered, officially unrecorded, over many thousands more.

The regulation and eventual abolition of rent did little to stimulate output. Wheat, oats and barley yields increased about twenty-five per cent between 1870 and 1930. But the fall in yields in these crops during the world war, when acreage had to be suddenly extended, implied that the main reason for this increase was the reduction in acreage, as grain came to be increasingly grown on the most suitable land. Even if the increased grain yields be attributed wholly to legislation, two decisive qualifications remain. The most striking increase in tillage yields occurred in potatoes, not as a result of legislation, but through the application of spraying techniques to prevent blight from the mid 1890s. Between

1876 and 1900 yields fell below three tons on seven occasions, after 1900 not once. Equally significantly, pasture output reflects no consistent response to legislation, either in density of stocking or in hay yields. Land legislation marked no 'new departure' in Irish agriculture. Neither the three Fs nor peasant proprietorship caused the hens to lay more eggs, and the peasants' reaction belied optimistic expectations. Little changed economically after 1881, indicating that rents had not proved an intolerable disincentive previously, nor, on the contrary, had they been an indispensable incentive, as landlords insisted, to goad a naturally indolent peasantry into reluctant activity. Price movements, not tenurial systems, dominated the volume and structure of agricultural output in the nineteenth century.

The Irish farmer showed himself a close calculator in more than his response to price changes. However intense his land hunger, it too sprang at least as much from calculation as from emotion. Only a handful of tenants purchased their properties under the Bright Clauses of the 1870 Land Act, because one-third of the money had to be paid down, and the annuity, 35 years at five per cent, frequently exceeded the rent. Farmers cooly spurned offers of leases in the early 1870s because lease holders were excluded from the provisions of the 1870 Act, the expense of solicitor's fees might equal a year's rent, and terms proved severe during a period of high prices. This reluctance to accept leases, however sensible in itself, places the tenants' alleged umbilical attachment to land in more realistic perspective. The tenant certainly wanted as much control as possible over his holding, but not at any price. The choice between peasant proprietorship, leases and annual tenancy was approached in a realistic rather than a romantic frame of mind. Only 731 tenants bought under the purchase provisions of the 1881 Act, which required a twenty-five per cent down payment, the balance to be repaid at five per cent over 35 years. The small Ashbourne Act in 1885, which advanced £5 million, augmented by a further £5 million in 1888, proved more successful. Twenty-five thousand tenants applied and the money was exhausted by 1891, because the repayment terms, 49 years at four per cent with no down payment, were far more attractive than previously. The 1891 Balfour Act imposed the same basic conditions, but hinged them around with so many qualifications for both tenants and landlords, who were to be paid not in cash but in land stock of fluctuating value, that despite an amending Act of 1896, only £13 of the £33 million made available was applied for. The Wyndham Act of 1903 was made compulsory in 1909 to deal with a small number of landlord recalcitrants, but landlords and tenants alike generally found the terms sufficiently satisfactory to reach amicable agreement. As the price ranged from 18½ to 27⅔ years purchase, somewhat above prevailing market prices, landlords got a very reasonable lump sum. The repayment terms, on the other hand, 68½ years at three per cent, averaging about twenty per cent below rent levels, with no down payment, seemed too attractive to the tenants to induce further hesitation. Only 70,000 holdings were purchased before 1903, nearly 300,000 under the Wyndham Act. Prior to 1903 many tenants showed by their actions that they shared Pat Shields' preference for a 'fair reduction' in rent to becoming a peasant proprietor by paying the equivalent of their present rent for thirty-five years.[32] Landlords were reluctant to sell in the early years, and many tenants doubtless could not afford the down-payment required by the 1870 and 1881 Acts. But the rate at which bank deposits increased, from £19 million in 1865 to £33 million in 1876 and again, from £33 million in 1890 to £43 million in 1903, suggests substantial rural savings. However much of this was earmarked for dowries, or for emigrant children, it undoubtedly existed, and its allocation indicates the order of peasant priorities.

If Land League predictions proved wildly optimistic, landlord prophecies of the disasters inherent in concessions to tenants plumbed even deeper depths of incomprehension. Land leaguers and landlords alike failed to understand the economics of agriculture, but the tenant leaders showed a much keener understanding of rural sociology than did landlord spokesmen. If the ascendancy represented, as it never tired of thinking, the intelligence as well as the wealth of the country – equating wealth with intelligence in typical traditional fashion – it kept its accomplishments discreetly concealed in justifying its *raison d'etre* at the supreme crisis in its history. The concensus landlord view was that peasant proprietorship 'would be the worst thing that could happen to the country . . . in a short time proprietors . . . would squander away their means, and get mortgages on their holdings, and things would get back to the worst'. Connacht landlords and agents, in particular, seemed to dwell in a fantasy world. The painfully honest, and even more painfully slow-witted Captain Boycott scaled his analytical peak in assuring Bessborough that 'every man in the country is in fear', but could only reply to the uncontemplated query 'if every man in the country is afraid, of whom are they afraid'? 'It is more than I can tell. That is my only answer'. Boycott revealed his remoteness from local reality in asserting that the agitation against him in 1879 began in August 'before it was known that it would be a bad year' although police in his own district noticed the blight in July. Col John Daley laboured to convince the commission that his tenants 'were pleased at being forced to pay their rents', while another landlord drew touching conclusions concerning the fidelity of his tenants who 'almost burst the walls of the office on rent day to get in to pay their rents – fighting to be the first to do so'. A more percipient landlord observer acknowledged that the alleged fear of large farmers to pay rents was 'a mere excuse', but this degree of insight into the society over which they presumed to preside was the exception rather than the rule. The most coherent landlord apologist, The Duke of Argyll, possessed so little grasp of Irish rural life that he actually predicted the consequence of the Land Act of 1881 would be a spate of sub-dividing and sub-letting, which only landlord determination had hitherto discouraged![33] If this represented the landlord gift to Irish social thought Land Leaguers could perhaps be forgiven for suspecting that Ireland might survive the loss of landlord intellect.

5 Home Rule and Unionism 1880–1914

Parnell and his party

A relative lull in activity occurred between 1882, when the land agitation calmed down, and the crescendo of excitement generated by the apparent imminence of home rule in 1886. Nevertheless, the intervening years proved of seminal importance in the political modernisation of Ireland, for they witnessed the emergence of the first modern political party in Irish history. If the Land League can be reckoned one of the most remarkable vehicles of agrarian agitation in nineteenth-century Europe, Parnell's party has some claim to be considered among the most remarkable political movements established in a primarily rural European society. In leadership, organisational efficiency, debating ability and political capacity it compared favourably with most continental contemporaries. In no European society, including England, did the transition from loosely organised, largely local groups to the tight central control of a national organisation occur so rapidly or effectively. The tragedy of the fall of Parnell was not only the tragedy of a great leader, but also the tragedy of a great party. It was precisely because the party had been hammered and honed into a superb political instrument that the eventual split proved so cathartic. The party was therefore doubly fortunate that it avoided until 1890 'the problem of the leadership' which exercises most political parties most of the time.

Parnell had already secured the leadership of the advanced wing of the Home Rule party before his remarkable band of lieutenants and contemporaries – John Dillon, William O'Brien, Tim Healy, John Redmond, Thomas Sexton, Tim Harrington – entered parliament in 1880 or in subsequent by-elections. Had Parnell not got his decisive, if short, head start, a bitter battle for leadership between able and ambitious men would hardly have been postponed until the 1890s. Parnell firmly scotched the only 'leadership crisis' of the 1880s, when Healy and Biggar contemplated seriously challenging his imposition of Captain O'Shea, who refused to take the party pledge, on Galway in 1886.

Parnell could rely on only 24 supporters out of 59 nominal Home Rulers in 1880. Support increased as it became clear that the future lay with him. Wavering members were won over, and public opinion responded so sympathetically to his appeal that in 1885, 86 Home Rule members (including T. P. O'Connor in Liverpool) who pledged to vote together, were returned. The receipt of a salary out of party funds – the first members at Westminster to be paid – reinforced their loyalty. Irish members, like their English colleagues, had previously frequently abandoned their independence for the spoils of office. Parnell's followers did not, despite being recruited from a generally poorer section of the community than previous Irish parties, for the type as well as the number of Nationalist M.P.s continued to change between 1880 and 1885. Seventy-three of 105 Irish M.P.s were landlords in 1868, including 37 Liberals. In 1874 23 of 59 Home Rulers were landed, in 1880 8 of 59, in 1885 only 5 of 86. The professions supplied eleven Irish M.P.s in 1868 compared with 29 Home Rulers alone in 1880 and 31 in 1885. Between 1880 and 1885 the number of farmers and shopkeepers, all Home Rulers, rose from 2 to 22, reflecting the rise of a new strata to potential political leadership. These changes likewise involved an increase in the number of Catholic M.P.s, from 37 in 1868 to 51 in 1874, 55 in 1880 and 75 in 1885. The representation of nationalist Ireland, in contrast to Unionist constituencies, was rapidly ceasing to be the plaything of birth, and becoming increasingly a function of political capacity in a fair field. Within the party the self-made men played a disproportionately prominent role. William O'Brien was the son of a respectable, but hardly affluent, clerk. Tim Healy, son of a poor law union clerk, and Thomas Sexton, son of a police constable, both began their careers as junior railway clerks. T. D. Sullivan worked as a house painter before turning to journalism, and T. P. O'Connor, son of a billiard saloon keeper, wrote his biography of Disraeli on the back of advertisement handbills distributed in London streets.

As national issues dominated the politics of Parnell's party, local roots became somewhat less significant as a springboard to political power. Many nationalist candidates were virtually unknown in their constituencies before selection. The local organisation generally accepted the nominees of the national party, which restricted the influence of the local clergy in choosing candidates. Although local considerations and candidates were to recover some influence after 1891, conditions never wholly reverted to the pre-1880 situation.

The massive enfranchisement of new voters in the third reform Act of 1884, which trebled the size of the electorate from about 230,000 to over 700,000, consolidated the base of this new type of political party. Westminster rarely conceded the full nationalist demand for suffrage extension during the nineteenth century. A Tory government, intent on denying formal participation in the political process to recalcitrant voters, actually halved the size of the electorate by disfranchising the 40/- freeholders in 1829. The Reform Act of 1850, mangled by the Lords, roughly doubled the electorate to 160,000. The second reform Act of 1867 excluded Ireland, but a grudging Irish measure in 1868 increased the electorate to about 230,000. The Redistribution Act of 1885 abolished the most obvious anomalies of the traditional system, the boroughs, where two per cent of the electorate returned fifteen per cent of the M.P.s and where the Secret Ballot Act of 1872 failed to reduce corruption as effectively as in the county constituencies. The Ballot Act may not, as Mr Hurst has forcefully argued, have made much difference to voting patterns. But it did encourage opponents of apparently entrenched landed dynasties to run candidates where previously the issue had generally been left uncontested. The eclipse of the dynasties outside the north-east – the Bruens and MacMurrough Kavanaghs in Carlow, the Powers in Wexford, the O'Conor Don in Roscommon, the Shirleys and Leslies in Cavan, Hamilton in Donegal – occurred in 1874 and 1880.

Parnell himself cared little about electoral systems, as long as they gave the right results. His ideal, in European terms, was probably Bonapartism, a plebiscitary dictatorship, with the voters duly returning massive 'yes' majorities whenever Parnell chose to consult them. He hesitated initially to support franchise reform, fearing that in a redistribution of constituencies Ireland would lose about 25 seats due to the decline in her population, which would more than outweigh the gain of 15 seats he expected from the extension of the franchise. The Whig element in the party, represented by the *Freeman's Journal*, realising than an extension would allow Parnellites to cut the ground from under their feet, were most unenthusiastic. Once Parnell was satisfied that Gladstone did not intend to reduce Irish representation he strongly endorsed the Reform Bill, which brought Ireland into electoral line with England. Whereas only 4·4 per cent of the population had the vote in 1884, compared with 9·7 per cent in England, after the Act sixteen per cent of the population, the same as in England, were entitled to vote. The extra half million voters by no means lacked previous electoral consciousness. Non-electors participated vigorously, if informally, in electioneering, either as intimidatory mobs or, probably more effectively, as customers of shopkeepers who had the vote and could be swayed by this reverse form of patronage. The discreetly phrased tributes of victorious candidates to non-electors 'who encouraged the doubtful and gave strength to the wavering' acknowledged the influence of the non-elector in pre-reform politics. The Reform Act nonetheless permitted a massive increase in formal electoral participation, and both the nationalist and unionist parties rapidly mobilised the new grassroots. The intensification of political consciousness and the improvement in electoral organisation stimulated a sharp increase in participation in local elections after 1881, once Parnell set his sights on capturing power at this level, and nationalists swept virtually the whole of municipal government outside the north-east. The National League, which succeeded the Land League as the main nationalist organisation after 1882, proved a highly efficient political machine, primarily reliant on constitutional tactics at the national and local levels.

The 1885 election completed the process, initiated in 1874, of eliminating English parties in southern Ireland. The Conservative party relied henceforth on the northeast. Ulster had usually contributed more than half the Conservative seats, eked out by a scatter of seats in the south wherever Protestants constituted a substantial proportion of the electorate. The small Liberal revival in 1880 may have owed something to Presbyterian tenants in Ulster defying their landlords in the secrecy of the polling booth, but the revival is to a large extent

Year	Conservatives	Liberals	Home Rulers	Total
1868	40	65	—	105
1874	32	12	59	103
1880	26	18	59	103
1885	18	—	85	103

deceptive. The bulk of Liberal votes in Donegal and Monaghan, where they made four of their six gains, came from home rule supporters. From 1885 the primacy of the Union issue rallied potential Liberal voters to the Conservative colours. Some liberal sentiment survived in the north-east though distinctly less than voting returns suggest, for Liberal candidates could usually rely on nationalist support when fighting Conservatives. Basically, the 1885 election established, with minor local variation, the electoral topography that persisted until 1918.

The Liberal Alliance

Parnell helped turn Gladstone out of office in June 1885, and directed the Irish in Britain to vote Tory at the general election in November. His judgement in playing the Tory card at this juncture reflected an astute reading of the political game. In June 1885 the Liberals were as uncommitted as the Conservatives to home rule. Gladstone's son announced his father's sensational conversion only on 17 December, after the election left 86 Parnellites holding the balance of power between 335 Liberals and 249 Conservatives. The ardour with which the Tories subsequently preached the imperial gospel, the vigour of their racialist rhetoric, should not obscure the fact that in mid-1885 some of the Tory leaders, including probably Salisbury himself, were poised to jump on the home rule bandwagon if this appeared likely to force the Liberal nag off the highway. Grassroots Tory sentiment might not have allowed Salisbury embrace home rule, for the backwoodsmen took racialist anti-Irish ideology seriously, and racism played a major role in Tory successes in crucial Lancashire constituencies, but a leader as complacent as Parnell of his command of his own party may have exaggerated the ability of English leaders to make their parties jump through the hoops.

Carnarvon, lord lieutenant during Salisbury's caretaker administration from June 1885 to January 1886, conveyed to Parnell the impression that the Tories were negotiable on home rule. As the Conservatives controlled the House of Lords they could reject a Liberal measure, and as the Liberals looked likely to win the election anyway, the conversion of either party to home rule seemed more likely if the nationalists held the balance of power. In addition, the Tory attitude towards denominational education and industrial protection was closer than that of the Liberals to the nationalist position. Parnell, then, had several convincing motives for urging the Irish in Britain to vote Tory.

Gladstone would have been happy to see Salisbury endorse home rule, partly because he genuinely believed in the principle, partly because Salisbury would probably split his party by taking any such initiative. Instead, the premature announcement of Gladstone's change of front in December 1885 effectively solved Salisbury's dilemma, convincing him that more electoral mileage, whatever his personal predilections – and it would be an exaggeration to consider him one of nature's celtophiles – would now be gained by playing the Orange card. In January 1886 the Tory leaders decided that Ireland must be held at all costs.

Despite the abruptness of his conversion, Gladstone brought most of his mesmerised party with him, but two vital minorities hived off to help the Tories kill the Home Rule Bill, by 341–311, in June 1886. The defection of the right wing under Hartington had been expected, but the defection of the left wing, under the formidable Joseph Chamberlain, effectively destroyed the bill. Home rule affronted both Chamberlain's social and political convictions. The vigorous Birmingham politician, already flirting with social imperialism, had not forgotten the patronising treatment he received during a tour of Ireland in 1885, and believed himself to have been deceived by Parnell in negotiations concerning a local government scheme for Ireland, conducted through the equally devious Captain O'Shea. British public opinion, which Parnell, intent on the power game at the top, had foolishly neglected, felt sufficiently committed to the conviction that English prestige depended on preserving the integrity of the United Kingdom to return Salisbury with a massive majority in the July 1886 general election.

Nevertheless, Nationalist political prospects on the morrow of the election appeared promising. The outstanding statesman of the age, and the progressive party in England, had adopted a hitherto excoriated principle, and it seemed likely to succeed next time round. Over two hundred British members supported a principle which got only one English vote when O'Connell raised it in 1834, and only ten when Isaac Butt attempted to distract the attention of the English members a decade before. Could the Parnellite momentum be maintained, some form of self-government for Ireland seemed assured in the foreseeable future. But if the Liberals were now committed to home rule, the Nationalists were equally tied to the Liberals unless English public opinion could be sufficiently weaned from imperialist principles to stimulate the Tories to an agonising reappraisal of their attitudes. The implications of the Liberal alliance were to remain concealed until the divorce crisis of 1890.

The Plan of Campaign

With Salisbury in office, and agricultural prices again falling – between 1881 and 1886 the land courts reduced rents twenty per cent, but the general Irish agricultural price level fell about thirty per cent – nationalist attention reverted once more to the land issue. The Plan of Campaign, devised by Tim Harrington and initiated in October 1886, involved offering the landlord what the tenants considered a fair rent and, if he refused, withholding the rents which would be used instead to support the evicted tenants. Although the papal condemnation of the Plan in 1888 proved ineffective, lack of money seriously weakened it, particularly once the landlords formed, with government support, their own consortium to counter tenant organisation with landlord organisation. By 1890 agreement through negotiation had been reached on 60 of the 116 estates affected by the Plan, tenant victory secured through confrontation on 24, defeat suffered on 15 while the struggle continued on 18 others.

The Fall of Parnell

The exposure in February 1889 of the Pigott forgeries, which the *Times* published in an attempt to implicate Parnell in the Phoenix Park murders of 1882, further increased his stature in Ireland and England. But in November 1890 the judgement in the divorce case of Captain and Mrs O'Shea sparked off two years of constitutional civil war. Popular opinion still clings to the emotionally satisfying myth that 'the bishops and the party, that tragic story made', that a great leader was hounded to his premature grave by a congenitally ungrateful people at the instigation of a vindictive clergy.

Parnell was not in fact brought down in Ireland on a moral issue. However disgusted the hierarchy may have been with the divorce court revelations, Parnell enjoyed such ascendancy over the country that the bishops didn't dare speak out on what was still generally considered a purely political issue. The party unanimously re-elected Parnell chairman on 25 November 1890, in full knowledge of the divorce judgement. It was not Ireland, but the nonconformist wing of the Liberal party in England that set the wheels in motion to bring down Parnell. Gladstone was prepared to accept Parnell's continued leadership, but the nonconformists threatened that they could not support an alliance with an adulterer, and Gladstone in effect delivered an ultimatum to the Irish party by intimating that Parnell's continued leadership would make it impossible for him to carry a united Liberal party on home rule. The issue now presented itself to the Home Rule party as Parnell versus the Liberal alliance, and, as the Liberals seemed certain to win the next election, this meant Parnell versus home rule. After protracted debates 45 members opted for home rule on 6 December, 27 for Parnell, who, having already wrecked any possibility of reconciliation with Gladstone by issuing a mendacious manifesto to the Irish people on 28 November concerning conversations with Gladstone which the latter immediately refuted, spurned all opportunities for compromise.

Parnell skilfully seized on the sole aspect that might be expected to gain him public sympathy in Ireland, the submission of the party to Gladstone's 'dictation'. His rivals, although frequently less than loath to extract electoral mileage from the moral issue, likewise laid prime emphasis on deference – the deference of the party to a dictator. Few more arrogant demands have ever been presented to a people than Parnell's insistence that Ireland abandon all chance of apparently imminent home rule simply to maintain his leadership, when he had been outmanoeuvred in the tactical struggle to retain control. His behaviour revealed the personality of a spoiled child. Ireland was his toy, and he arrogated the right to smash it at his whim. Suggestions that he might have 'temporarily' withdrawn were based on the false assumption that he placed the cause above himself. Granted Parnell's belief that his leadership was the only thing that mattered, compromise spelled defeat. His judgement did not deteriorate. He revealed in 1890–1 all the familiar flair of 1879–81, brilliantly seizing the slightest opportunities to turn the enemy's position.

But if it was important that Parnell should be defeated, it was also important that he fought. For there was an element of dictation involved in Gladstone's ultimatum, if no more than is inherent in any coalition situation. With no motive save ambition, without a spark of spontaneous generosity – his callous satisfaction at the death of Butt in 1879, as much his superior as a man as his inferior as a politician, dulls sympathy for even the tragic circumstances of his own early death – yet Parnell possessed the one political virtue which redeems all vices, courage. With his health visibly crumbling he dragged himself on miserable journeys from Brighton to brave vituperation where he had once been greeted like a God. Yet he never flinched as he contested every electoral inch. He had never given quarter, and, when circumstances changed, entirely through his own miscalculation, he asked for none. He left the legacy of a fighter to inspire nobler men than he to less selfish causes than his.

In five viciously fought by-elections all but one of Parnell's supporters, John Redmond in Waterford City, were defeated. Parnell died in October 1891 from illness contracted in the campaign, spared the humiliation of seeing only 9 Parnellites returned compared with 71 anti-

Parnellites in 1892. Despite the crushing defeat in terms of seats, his supporters won sufficient of the vote to suggest that his calculations in 1890 were by no means wholly unrealistic. Outside Catholic Ulster, which diverged sharply from the rest of the country, Parnellites performed creditably, winning thirty-eight per cent of the vote in 39 contested southern constituencies. They would hardly have won any of the uncontested constituencies, but they might have done better in them than in the six constituencies where they polled less than twenty per cent. They did not, for instance, contest Carlow, North Kilkenny or Sligo, where they lost by-elections earlier – but with twenty-eight, thirty-five and forty-three per cent of the vote respectively. On this basis it seems probable that about one-third of the nationalist electorate outside Ulster remained Parnellite after his death.

Had non-political considerations been decisive in bringing Parnell down in Ireland – as they were among the British nonconformists, still political primitives in this respect – one would have to concede that his fall marked a victory for traditionalistic theocratic forces claiming jurisdiction over a branch of secular activity which, in modern societies, must assert its autonomy. Both party and people, however, stood by Parnell in November 1890, as long as private morality was the only issue at stake, and the pattern of voting in the subsequent elections indicates the capacity of the vast majority of nationalists to distinguish between sacerdotal and secular.

At first sight the 1892 election returns seem to substantiate the Parnellite claim that they were beaten by the priests. Apart from Dublin, where they swept the four nationalist seats, and Waterford City, Parnellites won only four other constituencies. Throughout the country townsmen were generally held to have proved less amenable to clerical influence than their retarded country cousins. The unsuccessful Parnellite candidate in South Louth asserted that 'the independent men of Drogheda' had been overwhelmed by 'the docility of the country voters'.[34] In South Westmeath only the towns were Parnellite, and in North Westmeath, Mullingar accounted for almost half the Parnellite vote, prompting a Parnellite paper to claim that 'the towns were always in the van of Irish progress'.[35] In East Clare, Willie Redmond attributed his victory to the Ennis vote. Mathias Bodkin, who scraped home as an anti-Parnellite in North Roscommon, asserted that the towns were heavily Parnellite, and in closely contested North Meath, Trim was a Parnellite stronghold.[36]

Closer analysis of voting patterns during the century reveals, however, a more complex pattern of local loyalties. The electoral topography of the famous Tipperary by-election of 1869, indicates just how striking intra-constituency differences could be.[37]

Polling Booths	Rossa	Heron
Tipperary	497	10
Thurles	415	152
Cashel	152	122
Clonmel	45	129
Nenagh	34	609
Total	1143	1022

Before the Secret Ballot Act of 1872 sharp variations tended to be attributed to the relative influence of priests and landlords, but the persistence of similar patterns long after 1872, despite the reduction in the size of constituencies under the redistribution Act in 1885, suggests the significance of other factors in the creation of communal political consciousness, among which town-country distinctions, except in the case of the largest maritime centres, played a relatively minor role.

Before the Ballot Act increased the average number of polling centres from 4 to 20 per constituency, urban polling booths recorded overwhelmingly rural votes. Rossa's rural supporters outnumbered the anti-Rossa town voters in Cashel, and he owed his massive majority in Tipperary not to town voters, but, contrary to repeated assertions of concerted farmers' opposition to Fenianism, to the comfortable farmers of Clanwilliam barony.[38] Long after the Ballot Act many 'town' voters remained, in fact, rural. Of the 1,300 Parnellite voters recorded in an Ennis poll of 1,500 at least half must have been, on demographic grounds alone, 'Ennis, rural' in contrast to 'Ennis, urban'.[39] Bodkin qualifies his assertion about differences between urban and rural returns in North Roscommon by noting that 'political opinion was curiously and sharply divided through the division. In one district they were nearly all friends, in the next they were nearly all enemies . . .'[40] Boyle, the biggest town appears to have been anti-Parnellite, as was Sligo town, where an anti-Parnellite majority clinched a by-election victory against strong Parnellite rural support.[41] In three other Parnellite constituencies, South Roscommon, North Galway and West Clare, town-country distinctions were subsumed under the familiar pattern of sharp local variations.[42] In the North Kilkenny by-election, only Kilmanagh, the least urbanised district, recorded a Parnellite majority, while Grace's old Park, closest to Kilkenny town, polled anti-Parnellite, and Castlecomer, a mining centre, the largest town in the constituency, counted only 20 Parnellites compared with 900 anti-

Parnellites, the miners polling against Parnell to a man.[43] The town-country interpretation oversimplifies a more complex pattern of electoral behaviour.

The sharp cleavages in voting habits between localities with similar social structures and religious loyalties makes any generalisation concerning the relative significance of the various factors influencing the electorate exceptionally hazardous. It seems safe to suggest, however, that the priests, even when they presented a united front, could influence the voters only in the direction in which they wished to go. In the Tipperary by-election, the massive anti-Rossa vote in the north of the county was attributed to the fact that: 'from Birr to Birdhill priests and people, as of old, went together hand in hand'.[44] But the clergy in the rest of the county, initially equally anti-Rossa, were compelled by the temper of their flocks to judge discretion the better part of valour, and either 'went with the current' or, like Dr O'Neill 'who was the first to invite Mr Heron to the county' retreated into neutrality.[45] In 1879 the strongly 'clerical' James Daly delivered a slashing attack on the interferance of the Rev. Thomas MacHale, D.D. nephew of the archbishop of Tuam, in terms with which no Parnellite could quibble: 'a reactionary in principle, he has no respect for individual liberty, and he claims the right to direct not only the religious but the political opinions of those over whom he asserts jurisdiction'.[46] When the revered archbishop himself opposed the Westport meeting on 8 June 1879, a 'voice in the crowd' complacently assured the meeting that MacHale 'had got into bad company'.[47]

In 1892, there is little evidence that even the unprecedentedly vigorous clerical intervention influenced many voters to change their minds. Bishop Nulty of Meath gave drunkards and prostitutes a rare episcopal leg-up by exalting them above Parnellites, but this did not deter forty-eight per cent of Meath voters from asserting their preference for traditional theology. The results of the Meath elections were annulled on grounds of clerical intimidation. The voting patterns remained almost identical, however, in the new contests in 1893, though the clergy this time displayed some self-control. In Roscommon, Bishop Gillooly had the mortification of seeing South Roscommon return a Parnellite, while Bodkin only nudged home in North Roscommon. In North Galway, the archbishop of Tuam found that his excommunication of the Parnellites involved in disrupting a clerical election meeting left the voters unimpressed.[48] Clare provides a particularly interesting pointer to the limits of clerical influence, widely and wildly exercised in East Clare, much less active in West Clare.[49] Yet Parnellites won both seats, suggesting that clerical influence made only a marginal difference to the overall result.

The failure of Tim Healy to create a clericalist party in the following decade – South Kerry, overwhelmingly anti-Parnellite in 1892, delivered a crushing rebuff to Healy's candidate in 1895, and only 3 of his 15 supporters were returned in 1900 – confirms the limited electoral influence of the clergy. The next major electoral struggle, between the Home Rule party and Sinn Féin, in 1917–18, emphasised yet again the limits of clerical influence. On this occasion, in contrast to 1892, the Church was publicly fragmented. The generation gap loomed as large between curates and parish priests as between fathers and sons.[50] The support of Dr Foley, bishop of Kildare and Leighlin, could not prevent the home rule candidate withdrawing in Carlow, and, despite being proposed by Dr Hoare, bishop of Ardagh and Clonmacnoise, J. F. Farrell was crushed in Longford. A little incident in Mayo captures the essence of the political relationship between Catholic clergy and laity. A fair day crowd in Straide, birth and burial place of Michael Davitt, refused a hearing to a Sinn Féin contingent from Castlebar led by Fr Meehan, C.C. 'Has it come to the time' he cried, 'when an Irish Catholic priest will be refused a hearing in Mayo?' He was met by a chorus of protests, and told: 'when you are on the right side we will hear you'.[51] 'When you are on the right side' may serve as a succinct summary of the political power of the priest before 1918.

Moral Force Unionism

In 1893 Gladstone guided the second Home Rule Bill through the Commons, but the Tory-dominated Lords rejected it. With the Tories in power from 1895 to 1905, and the Liberals returned in 1906 with a sufficiently large majority to ignore home rule, the Nationalist party did not again hold the balance of power until 1910. Several struggled to succeed Parnell after 1891, but no one could replace him. The anti-Parnellite leaders, John Dillon, Tim Healy and William O'Brien, jockeyed for position with each other and with John Redmond, leader of the Parnellite rump. O'Brien, disgusted with his failure to profit from the internal squabbling, seized the opportunity proffered by the potato failure of 1897, which yet again created distress in Connacht, to establish the United Irish League in 1898 to concentrate agitation on the land issue once more. The U.I.L. aroused such widespread, if ephemeral, enthusiasm, enrolling 50,000 members within two years, that the Parliamentary party, virtually in self-defence, rallied around the Parnellite, Redmond, in 1900, and succeeded in asserting its primacy over the maverick League in 1902. The League henceforth became synonymous with the party machine, but it deserves to be remembered as the final mass movement in Irish history concerned primarily with the land issue. Henceforth the increasingly widespread use of the spray, the most effective prophylactic against social revolution in modern Ireland, took the potato out of politics.

A major bone of contention between the contending home rule factions was the extent to which they should support moral force unionism – ameliorative measures introduced with the express purpose of 'killing home rule by kindness'. John Dillon, in particular, remained extremely suspicious of several measures aimed at solving longstanding grievances. Arthur Balfour hardly intended to keep his promise of 'repression as stern as Cromwell's' when he became chief secretary in 1887. His 'repression' resulted in little more than William O'Brien losing his pants in jail and three people losing their lives in Mitchelstown when police opened fire on a crowd, a derisory haul which must have left Cromwell turning in his desecrated grave. Balfour probably intended his promise of 'concessions as great as Mr Parnell and anyone else can desire', short of home rule, to be taken more seriously. Convinced that Irish nationalism was 'born in the peasant's cot, where men forgive if the belly gain' he concentrated on improving economic conditions as an antidote to the home rule virus. Moral force unionism was based on the assumption that every native had his price, but Balfour's grasp of the functioning of that particular price system, and his choice of murder weapons for home rule, betrayed a certain lack of sophistication. His light railway schemes, pushed through in response to the potato failure of 1890 in the west, made little contribution to the local economies. He established the Congested Districts Board in 1891 to deal with the poverty stricken west. The congested districts were defined to comprise initially one-sixth of the country and one-tenth of the population. By 1910 the area under the Board's auspices had been extended to embrace one-third of the country and a quarter of the population.

The Board's main function soon came to be the purchase of estates under the land legislation, and their reallocation to existing tenants. In its purchase and redistribution policy the Board dithered between a variety of alternatives. It divided estates in the first instance among existing tenants, allocating anything left over to the poorest remaining tenants in the locality, but excluding landless labourers. Once it allocated the estates in east Connacht to the local tenants, nothing remained, short of breaking up the ranches, for the even more poverty-stricken farmers further west, only a handful of whom were resettled outside their own localities. Ultimately, the majority of tenants were simply confirmed on their existing holdings. Only about 16,000, less than ten per cent of tenants in the congested districts, had the value of their holdings seriously affected by the Board's actions, although over 2,000,000 acres were purchased by 1923 under the provisions of the land acts. The Board claimed credit for spreading the use of the potato spray. But all tenants, inside or outside the congested districts, proved alert to innovations connected with potato cultivation. The rapidity of the response, as striking in the west as in the east, to the immunity of the champion potato from blight in 1880, when the proportion of the potato acreage under champions rose from twenty-seven to sixty-three per cent in a single year, suggests that tenants were more than capable of keeping abreast of relevant developments in this area without any promptings from the Board.

The attempts to foster lace-making, knitting, weaving and fishing proved an expensive waste of time and money. Few of the sponsored projects survived competition, and the dribble of earnings – by 1913, £166,000 per annum from fishing, £30,000 from 'industries' – contributed less than two per cent of the income of the congested districts. The Board adopted the disastrous policy of creating uneconomic work which was bound to disappear the moment support was withdrawn. Had the capital invested in uneconomic projects in the west been intelligently invested in the east, not only would the east have developed more rapidly, but the inevitable movement from the west might gradually have been diverted from emigration to internal migration. Massively subsidising the west simply ensured that those unable to find employment in that area had then nowhere to turn, because of the failure of the east to expand as rapidly as it might otherwise have done. Within the congested districts themselves the Board actually attempted to locate projects in the most backward areas, wholly lacking any basis for further development, so that they constituted little more than a polite form of unemployment relief. The local Catholic clergy enthusiastically supported the Board's endeavours but their attempt to improve living standards probably encouraged the emigration it was designed to reduce. The aspirations aroused exceeded the ability to satisfy them.

After 1891 the congested districts continued to experience exceptionally high emigration, as the Board failed to reduce the differential between eastern and western emigration rates. However complacently the Board's officials predicted in 1892 that they could 'double output' in western agriculture, nothing of the sort happened. No significant change occurred in the relative trends of agricultural output between the congested district and the rest of the country during the thirty-two years of the Board's existence. The Board's promise, in short, generally far exceeded its performance.

Among the few who realised the inadequacy of the Board's policy was one of its first members, Horace Plunkett. Observing, like many others, that the unreliability of the quality of Irish butter, notoriously the most unpredictable on the English market, restricted its sale and reduced its price, Plunkett concluded that the farmers must be taught self-help. After overcoming initial scepticism between 1889 and 1894 concerning his alien notion that honesty was the best policy in describing their wares, and that customers valued cleanliness and freshness, interest developed sufficiently to justify his establishing the Irish Agricultural Organisation Society in 1894. By 1914 one thousand societies were in existence, with an annual turn-over of £3·5 million. The co-operative movement centered around the local creamery, which attempted to cut out the middlemen merchants and to assess the real quality of the farmers' butter. It succeeded only partly, however, in emulating the standards established by continental competitors. Cow and heifer numbers increased from 1·36 million in 1889 to 1·64 million in 1914. But the increase was concentrated into two short periods, from 1889 to 1891, before the co-operative movement could have exerted any influence, and again after 1906, when a decline in the profitability of dry cattle led to a relative improvement in dairying prospects. The gap between Irish and Danish prices on the London market remained striking, and it appears to have been the general rise in world prices which dragged Irish prices in their wake.

Plunkett's own farming experience on a Meath estate and on an American ranch did not prepare him to grasp fully the nature of social relationships in rural Irish communities. Agricultural credit banks, in which the members guaranteed loans to one another, formed an important component of the co-operative movement, but, as credit worthiness varied with the value of the farm, loans were naturally made to men with the most security. Those in least need managed to borrow most on the basis of local communal farmer guarantees. By helping to widen differences in income between larger and smaller farmers, the co-operative movement fostered dissension and jealously within the rural community.

It was partly Plunkett's groping realisation of the necessity to impress on sceptical smaller farmers the advantages of cooperation that induced him to canvass the establishment of the department of Agriculture and Technical Instruction, and to become its first vice-president in 1899. The department, however, made little immediate impact. It failed to translate the information it assiduously collected into terms intelligible to the farmer, and tended to lose sight of the economic wood for the technical trees. It was plagued by political troubles, for pressure from the Nationalist party persuaded the Liberal government to sack Plunkett, a Unionist, in 1907. His successor, T. W. Russell, a political appointment, never measured up to the job. Neither did T. P. Gill, an ex-Nationalist M.P., Plunkett's unfortunate, if well-intentioned choice as secretary to the department in 1899. It is possible that, even if the cooperative movement and the department of agriculture did not improve the relative position of Irish farmers in the English market, they may have prevented it from deteriorating further. But the increasing prosperity of rural Ireland in the two decades before the first world war owed far more to the potato spray and international agricultural price rises then to either cooperation or government policy.

The Local Government Act of 1898 established five organs of local administration. County and city councils became responsible for administrative and financial affairs, rural and urban district councils for housing and public health, and boards of guardians for poor relief and medical charities. The Act promised to be an important measure of political modernisation. By replacing the grand juries with elected county councils it broke the landlord stranglehold on local affairs. John Redmond considered it the most important initiative in Irish politics in his generation, in that it helped prepare nationalists for the responsibility of self-government by giving them an opportunity of acquiring administrative experience. But in fact the Act became the first major example of the potential conflict between political and social modernisation, for the new system soon became as big a byword as the old for corruption. As the Act did not provide for competitive entrance examinations, appointments were virtually by favouritism only, and non-canvassing automatically disqualified. It later took the Free State government years to clean out the augean stable of corruption and confusion that flourished under it. Virtually the only important contribution of the new councils was to rapidly increase the number of labourers' cottages from 16,000 in 1900 to 60,000 in 1908, finally sweeping the wretched cabins from the face of the land. It was little wonder, given the prevailing appointments system, that, contrary to the complacent Redmondite assurances, few men of vision or ability graduated from the local councils to the national scene.

The fourth major problem 'solved', though under Liberal rather than Conservative auspices, was the university question. James Bryce, the Liberal chief secretary, attempted to establish a new Catholic college within the University of Dublin, but Trinity College successfully opposed this proposal. Bryce's successor, Augustine Birrell, then embraced an alternative scheme, incorporated in the Irish Universities Act of 1908. This created a new university college in Dublin, officially non-denominational but with a predominantly Catholic teaching body. It was linked with the Queen's colleges in Cork and Galway as part of the National University, leaving Trinity College to enjoy its inheritance unmolested, and conferring independent university status on Queen's College, Belfast. The Act made only miserable financial provision for the new university, and the First World War soon intervened disastrously to increase the building costs of University College, Dublin and to condemn its administrators to a hand-to-mouth existence, which precluded whatever possibility existed of establishing a university of genuine international calibre. Money was not, however, the only problem. Standards were set exceptionally low, and little emphasis put on research in the social sciences so crucial to solving the problems of Irish society. Apart from a few isolated individuals, the members of the new university apparently entertained from the outset little ambition to make a major impact on either the quality of Irish life or the world of international scholarship. The threat of competition failed, in turn, to rouse Trinity College from its slumbers as 'the silent sister' of Oxford and Cambridge. In the short run, the new university probably reinforced rather than reduced the existing inequalities of opportunity in Irish society, for the low standards allowed less gifted children of the middle classes acquire a degree, which increased the status differential between them and clever but poor children, unable to secure a university place through lack of scholarships.

The Congested Districts Board, the Department of Agriculture and Technical Instruction, the Local Government Act, and the Universities Act made little contribution to the modernisation of Irish society. They were all major missed opportunities. They exposed with repeated clarity the bankruptcy not only of the official mind but of the Home Rule party, when confronted with issues other than the nature of Anglo-Irish relations.

Physical Force Unionism

By 1905 'kindness' had proved much too blunt a murder weapon for Orange tastes. Unionists had captured the princely total of one extra Irish seat since 1887, and the danger seemed to be, from a unionist viewpoint, that some of the Anglo-Irish, judging from their attempts to find common ground with nationalists on the land question in 1904–5, might come to think of themselves as Irish first and Anglo second. The Ulster Unionist council

was established in 1905 to counter the threat of conciliation breaking out in Southern Ireland and to ensure that
the imminent return of the Liberals to power should not
damage Ulster Protestant interests. Home rule receded
as an immediate possibility when the Liberals won a
landslide victory in 1906, but became a live issue once
more when the general election of February 1910 left the
Nationalists holding the balance of power. The Liberals
abolished the Lords' veto on legislation in the Parliament
Act of 1911, which permitted the Lords to obstruct a bill
for a maximum of two years, after which it automatically
became law. This removed the last constitutional safe-
guard for the Unionists, who had hitherto relied on the
Lords' veto to frustrate the Commons' wishes, as in 1893.

Sir Edward Carson, a powerful orator and shrewd
tactician, already a distinguished Tory, was elected leader
of the Irish Unionists in 1910. His second in command,
James Craig, a millionaire distiller who fought with
conspicuous bravery in the Boer War, concealed an
astute political mind and considerable administrative
ability beneath massively immobile features. Carson and
Craig constituted one of the most formidable partner-
ships in Irish history.

The Scotch-Irish subjective sense of separate identity –
the ultimate criterion of nationality – drew sustenance
from a history, language, culture and economy undeni-
ably different from those which nationalists choose to
consider essentially Irish. Racialism, articulated in religious
idiom, dominated Scotch-Irish hostility to home rule.
That home rule meant Rome rule was, for the average
Ulster Protestant, conclusive condemnation of any tam-
pering with the union. Rome rule conjured up the night-
mare of a native rising for a settler community. Economic
factors merely reinforced racial pride. It was as vulgar a
unionist error to assume that Belfast prospered because
of the union as it was a nationalist error to assume that the

southern Irish economy decayed because of it. But both sides clung in ignorant passion to their conflicting interpretations. Belfast manufacturers imported the bulk of the raw materials for the shipping and linen industries. They assumed that a home rule parliament would impose tariffs, increasing the costs of Belfast's indispensable raw materials, pricing her products out of their vital exports markets, crippling Ulster's industrial economy. They had reaped the fruits of free trade, prospering in open competition against all-comers on a world market. If the rest of Ireland couldn't measure up to international standards, this, to successful Belfast businessmen, simply reflected the native incapacity of the Celt to master the industrial virtues. Why should they be penalised to succour lesser breeds? The economic argument thus fused into the racial syndrome.

In every generation the Protestant people had asserted their right to racial supremacy. Several times in the previous century they had asserted it in riots and religious revivals. The riots of 1857 were followed hot-foot by 'the second evangelical awakening' which swept through Ulster, en route from America to Britain, in 1859. The awakening found expression in a conviction so intense of God's grace that it sometimes resulted in physical prostration, in mass conversions of 'sinners', and in an intoxicating experience of personal redemption – as one repentant sinner who ambitiously defied 'the townland of Brough-shane to produce my equal in profligacy or any sin whatever' modestly reassured his alarmed audience 'I stand before you this day a monument to the perfect grace of God'. Critics of the revival complained that mass meetings consisted of girls issuing ecumenical invitations to kiss-ins, and of excited ladies experiencing exhilarating visions of hell with a pope dancing on a red-hot griddle and another pope cutting turf – as Paddy's national fuel, peat was particularly appropriate for stoking the satanic furnaces. Supporters of the revival indignantly denied the scurrilous rumours of kissing.

As riot and revival appealed to the same psychology, 'Roaring' Hugh Hanna 'this noted doctor of divinity and laws', fresh from his triumphs in the 1857 riots, played a prominent role in the awakening in Belfast. The revival, however, failed to provide more than momentary diversion from sterner joys, and riot shortly resumed its sovereign sway. Each generation, indeed almost each year, was baptised anew in the faiths of their fathers. The Belfast riots of 1864 claimed 7 dead and 150 wounded. The quiet years between 1872 and 1880 accounted for 10 dead and 375 wounded throughout the province. In 1886, 32 died and at least 400 were wounded in Belfast. These were no petty squabbles, and Belfast riots alone accounted for more fatalities than all the nationalist risings of the nineteenth century.

Not until the threat of home rule crystallised in 1886 did the Orange Order find it necessary to extend its predominantly workingclass membership to incorporate the overwhelming majority of middle and upper classes. It was a historic moment, the first occasion in European history when traditional elitist conservatism capitulated to the radical right. Respectable Protestant society, having hitherto evinced a superior distaste for the vulgarity of workingclass Orangeism, now subscribed in droves to the Orange Order. Already in January 1886, within a month of Gladstone's conversion to home rule, the establishment of the Ulster Loyalist Anti-Repeal Union began unionist mobilisation. It is a travesty of the dedication of grassroots unionists to imply, as nationalist propagandists were prone to do, that they were prodded into activity against the Home Rule Bill only when Lord Randolph Churchill played the Orange card in February 1886 by bequeathing to Belfast the slogan 'Ulster will fight and Ulster will be right'. Lord Randolph's performance concerns the connoisseur of Tory constitutional theory rather than the student of Orange convictions. For however disloyal unionist leaders may occasionally have been to Orange principles, the great dumb faithful masses always stood firm. Orangemen did not need to be told either that they were right or that they would fight.

The 1886 riots were not sparked off by Churchill's incitement, but by a characteristic local dispute when one Patrick Murphy, a Catholic dock labourer, revealed to a Protestant colleague a vision of home rule culminating in a one hundred per cent Orange unemployment rate. Murphy's threat crystallised an endemic Orange fear, and, through the familiar series of chain reactions, led to the worst riots of the century. Murphy reflected faithfully enough the mentality of many Belfast Catholics, mirror-images of their Orange brethren, who simply reversed the denominational adjectives and, in their ideal world, denied equality of opportunity to Protestants as emphatically as Orangemen denied it to them. Catholics of this vintage were mobilised by the Ancient Order of Hibernians, revitalised under Joe Devlin after 1886. Devlin, a consummate machine politician, gradually extended his sectarian grip over the Catholic community in Ulster and acquired considerable influence within the Home Rule party outside Ulster.

Nationalist interpretation of popular unionist opposition to home rule rose no higher than simple conspiracy theory. Home rulers and republicans alike simply assumed that unionists were deluded victims of a false consciousness cunningly implanted by English propaganda. Socialists like James Connolly, who enjoyed some trade union but no political success in Belfast in 1910–12, attributed Protestant workingclass unionism exclusively to employer exploitation of religious differences. Conspiracy theory, nationalist or socialist, painted a contemptuous picture of the unionist in the street as a stupid dupe incapable of appreciating his real interests. When John Redmond protested his abhorrence of the 'two nations in Ireland' theory he conveniently claimed the right, which he fiercely resisted when exercised by unionist politicians on nationalists, to define the Scotch-Irish out of existence.

It is true that Redmond was prepared to make what he considered generous concessions towards Scotch-Irish susceptibilities, virtually amounting to 'home rule within home rule', as long as the Ulster unionists acknowledged ultimate allegiance to the sovereignty of a Dublin parliament. But Redmond forgot that it was not equality, but superiority, the Orangeman claimed as his birthright. And home rule, however generous the 'special considerations' for unionists, certainly threatened a fatal blow at the master-race syndrome. This was the essence of the Ulster question, and as long as the Scotch-Irish were prepared to fight in defence of their ascendency no peaceful solution was possible. Occasional deviations from the straight and narrow of unionist orthodoxy – like T. H. Sloan's Independent Orange movement – on which nationalists and socialists seized with pathetic determination to rescue unionists from their deluded selves, were more likely to represent reactions against official unionist 'softness' on Catholics than the reverse.

Home rule leaders virtually ignored the Ulster question until after the passing of the third Home Rule Bill through the Commons in January 1913. They took at its face value the reiterated British assertion that parliament was the ultimate court of appeal. That, they had been taught, was the genius of the British constitution. What they should have foreseen, after Lord Randolph's performance in 1886, was that the Tories would contemptuously reject the decision of parliament and resort to the threat of physical force. Bonar Law, who became Conservative leader after Balfour's retirement in 1911, provided theoretical justification for all physical force enthusiasts when asserting, with Bismarckian resonance, 'there are things stronger than parliamentary majorities' and when announcing in July 1912 that he could imagine 'no lengths of resistance to which Ulster can go in which I should not be prepared to support them'. On 28 September 1912 nearly a quarter of a million Protestant men pledged in the Solemn League and Covenant to resist home rule by any means. The Scotch-Irish yielded nothing to nationalists in the tenacity of their historical memories. The document was modelled on a sixteenth-century covenant, the traditional Presbyterian technique for reminding God whose side he was on. Clergymen of all Protestant persuasions played prominent roles in organising the covenant, for however much ministers might appear to dominate their congregations they, like their Catholic counterparts, had to follow their flocks or be left stranded.

Brilliantly though the Unionists played the political game, inside and outside parliament, they achieved only partial success. The fundamental unionist objective was to preserve not only Ulster, but Ireland, from home rule. Compelled to abandon this objective, they next demanded the exclusion of the nine counties of Ulster from the bill. Reminded that Nationalists had a majority in five of the nine counties, they then decided to claim as much of Ulster as they could be sure of holding, reassured by the silly but widespread belief that Southern Ireland could not survive economically without the north-eastern counties. Partition schemes were tossed about, mainly by English liberals struggling to escape from the dilemma. These generally envisaged an 'Ulster' ranging from four to six counties, or, very sensibly, abandoned the artificial county criterion to find a border which took account of local loyalties. The nationalists, refusing to contemplate partition at all, had no contingency plans, and ignored the opportunity for effective manoeuvre on the precise location of the border in their refusal to concede the principle. They thus squandered the possibility of a four-county border, as proposed by the Liberal Agar-Robartes in June 1912, which Carson, if only for tactical reasons, accepted.

The Ulster Volunteers, established in January 1913, soon enrolled 100,000 members. Their determination to resist home rule by force, initially reliant on small imports of arms in 1913, derived realistic substance from the superbly executed gunrunning at Larne and Donaghadee in April 1914, when 24,600 guns and 3,000,000 rounds of ammunition were imported from Germany. The previous month unionist officers at the Curragh requested not to be ordered to march against Ulster. It was a supreme irony that it should have taken the Curragh mutiny to preserve nationalist self-respect. It would have formed an ironic commentary on the proclaimed ideals of nationalism if a quarter of the population were to be terrorised into joining a home rule state by the British army. Tories, having preached law and order throughout the nineteenth century, now preached violence and sedition. Nationalists, having denounced coercion throughout the nineteenth century, now clamoured for the coercion of 'Ulster'. Circumstances alter cases!

The formation of the Ulster Volunteers and their acquisition of arms marks a decisive turning point in Irish history. By bringing the gun back into politics, Orangemen paved the way for the triumph of forces long gestating in southern society.

6 Anglicisation or Modernisation? 1892–1918

'The necessity for de-anglicising Ireland'

The election of 1892 savagely debased the currency of political debate. Jasper Tully, proprietor of the *Roscommon Herald*, anti-Parnellite M.P. for Leitrim, provided a representative sample of the quality of the campaign invective in castigating Luke Hayden, proprietor of the rival *Roscommon Messenger*, Parnellite M.P. for South Roscommon, as 'that poor unfortunate fool . . . a man who can barely read and write, who cannot spell properly, and is seldom tolerably sober. He is a fitting, greasy type of the intelligence of the ignorant, besotted districts that elected him. Fortunately he can do no harm to no one but himself'. Many readers, even among those insensitive to double negatives, could not long stomach this level of polemic. In November 1892, only a few months after the election, Douglas Hyde, son of a Roscommon rector, attempted to shift the focus of discussion from politics to 'identity' in a lecture to the National Literary Society, 'The Necessity for de-Anglicising Ireland'.

Hyde believed that by imitating the English 'in our dress, literature, music, games, and ideas only a long time after them and a vast way behind', and by abandoning the Irish language after the famine, 'we have at last broken the continuity of Irish life'. He predictably urged support for native music and for Gaelic games, as fostered by the Gaelic Athletic Association founded in 1883 to encourage native sports and discourage cricket, soccer, hockey and rugby, stigmatised as garrison games. 'Let us', he further exhorted, 'set our faces against this aping of English dress, and encourage our women to spin and our men to wear comfortable free suits of their own . . .' Knee-breeches he extolled as the ideal native (male) dress. 'Perhaps the principal point of all', he continued, 'is the necessity for encouraging the use of Anglo-Irish literature instead of English books, especially instead of English periodicals. We must set our face sternly against penny dreadfuls, shilling shockers, and still more the garbage of vulgar English weeklies like *Bow Bells* and the *Police Intelligence*. Every house should have a copy of Moore and Davis'.

Apart, therefore, from his insistence on the importance of reviving the Irish language, Hyde derived his inspiration primarily from Anglo-Irish rather than Gaelic concepts of Ireland. Moore and Davis owed little to native literary tradition, substituting sentiment for the sharp edge of sardonic self-criticism characteristic of the Irish mind before Anglo-Irish bowdlerisation. Hyde's vision of 'traditional' Ireland, his concept of the 'continuity' that had been broken, simply involved the imposition of his boyhood recollections on 2,000 years of history. He equated virtually everything existing in his youth with 'real' Irish, even though it may well have been an earlier import from England, and denounced virtually every development during his adult years as 'anglicisation'. In his zeal for kneebreeches, for instance, he came close to proclaiming 'down with trousers' as the battle cry of his brave new Ireland. Hyde in fact populated his ideal Ireland with a nation of stage-Irishmen, mimicking reality in Irish instead of English. He dreaded the threat of a modernised Gaelic Ireland as intensely as the prospect of a modernised anglicised Ireland. The whole infra-structure of modernisation appalled him, and he assumed that the Irish could not survive in a modernised world. They should therefore, unlike every other European people, opt out from the modernisation process and continue to dwell in a mythical world of kneebreeches, free suits, and martial ballads. Characteristically, he said virtually nothing about 'Irish ideas', devoting more attention to dress than to thought. His own analysis plumbed fresh intellectual depths as it reeled from comparison to crazy comparison: 'we will become, what, I fear, we are largely at present, a nation of imitators, the Japanese of Western Europe . . .' – selecting, with instinctive confusion, a society which succeeded more than any other in combining technical innovation with a distinctive way of life. He urged the Irish to imitate nineteenth-century Greece, which abandoned German and restored the Greek language after achieving independence in 1830 – oblivious to the fact that as Greek had always remained the vernacular, German having gained currency only in court circles, no restoration was necessary!

Hyde's confusion derived mainly from his equation of modernisation with anglicisation. He grossly exaggerated the threat of anglicisation by failing to distinguish the specifically English from the generally modern. Except in the one important, but not crucial, matter of language, Ireland was no more anglicised in 1892 than in 1848. Since the Tudor conquest, land and religion formed the two major recurring topics of debate between conquerors and conquered. Both government and colonists long attempted to impose English ideas of property and God, not always easily distinguishable, on the natives. It was in Hyde's excoriated nineteenth century that England conceded defeat in these two crucial areas. The transformation of the tenurial system, the euthanasia of the aristocracy, marked a major victory for native values – all the more remarkable in that these values were themselves transmuted through the centuries. The native mind responded to the English challenge not by clinging blindly to the old concepts, but by creating new 'native' values, which it then compelled the conqueror to recognise as 'immemorial tradition', and which even the Scotch-Irish settlers adopted. The disestablishment of the Church of Ireland – Hyde's Church – in 1869 represented yet another reverse for the official English *Weltanschauung*, another triumph for native ideas. In the later nineteenth century the contrasts between the role of religion in Irish and English life increased considerably. The intensity of institutional devotion actually increased in Ireland while it declined in England. The continuing viciousness of sectarian politics in the north-east, despite the gradual mellowing of sectarian animosities in England, began to mark off the Scotch-Irish from the British way of life. What Hyde mistook for anglicisation – the proliferation of government boards, the diffusion of popular literature, the growth of mass consumption – simply reflected the administrative and cultural requirements of mass society, developments occurring more or less simultaneously in all European countries, without in the least involving their 'anglicisation'.

In 1893 he became founder-president of the Gaelic League, which achieved its initial objective of arresting the decline of the language, but failed to revive it as a vernacular. It helped make Irish a widely taught school subject, by pressurising the Liberal government to rein-troduce in 1906 the school fees for the teaching of Irish which the Tories had abolished the previous year. By 1909 about 3,000 of the 9,000 primary schools were teaching Irish, compared with fewer than a hundred a decade earlier.

Hyde's endearing personality and patent sincerity have disguised his ideological isolation within the broader Gaelic movement. Hyde found himself among the lunatic fringe of 'traditionalists', bypassed by active modernisers in the Irish Republican Brotherhood and in James

Connolly's Irish Socialist Republican Party, founded in 1896. Sceptical of Hyde's obsession that trousers were an exclusively English contribution to civilisation – rejecting his glib equation of modernisation with anglicisation – these movements refused to seek refuge from the twentieth century in Hyde's retreat from reality, but instead determined to capture reality for their respective visions of Gaelic Ireland.

The preoccupation of 'Irish-Irelanders' with legitimising their aspirations by invoking alleged precedents from the celtic mists has misled some observers into portraying them as simple reactionaries. In fact, far from being prisoners of the past, the modernisers created the past in their image of the future. Those most intent on accelerating the pace of modernisation, notably Patrick Pearse and James Connolly, most insistently appealed to the legitimising authority of history.

Pearse

Patrick Pearse, son of a radical English monumental sculptor and an Irish mother, was born in Dublin in 1879. After graduating in law from the Royal university he abandoned 'the most evil of all professions' to found his own secondary schools, St Enda's and St Ita's. Pearse's language gives commentators who portray him as the personification of the reaction against modernisation, considerable excuse for their misunderstanding. 'Ye men and peoples, burn your books on rent theories and land values and go back to your sagas' is not the most familiar text of the gospel of modernisation. But closer scrutiny suggests that Pearse mobilised the sagas as weapons to achieve his goal of modernisation without anglicisation.

Pearse sought the clue to the development of the individual personality, his abiding preoccupation in education, and developed his most sustained analysis of the nature of the ideal society in an examination of the Irish educational system, 'the murder machine'. He denounced the intermediate education system introduced in 1879 as 'the most evil thing that Ireland has ever known', because 'it took absolutely no cognisance of the differences between localities, of the differences between urban and rural communities, of the differences springing from a different ancestry, Gaelic or Anglo-Saxon. Every school must conform to a type – and what a type! . . . precisely the same textbooks are being read tonight in every secondary school and college in Ireland. Two of Hawthorne's *Tanglewood Tales* with a few poems in English, will constitute the whole literary pabulum of three-quarters of the pupils of the Irish secondary school during this twelve months. The teacher who seeks to give his pupils a wider horizon in literature does so at his peril . . .'. In contrast to a factory concept of regimented education, Pearse propounded his ideal system in terms of medieval Gaelic fosterage customs: 'it was always the individual inspiring, guiding, fostering other individuals: never the state usurping the place of father or fosterer, dispensing education like a universal provider of ready-mades, aiming at turning out all men and women according to regulation patterns . . . it seems to me that there has been nothing nobler in the history of education than this development of the old Irish plan of fosterage under a Christian rule, when to the pagan ideals of strength and truth there were added the Christian ideals of love and humility'.

Pearse's concept of fosterage has been the butt of many a historian wit. But Pearse, more practical than his critics, anticipated the wits: 'I can imagine how blue Dr Hyde, Mr Yeats and Mr MacNeill would look if their friends informed them that they were about to send them their children to be fostered. But, at least, we can bring the heroes and seers and scholars to the schools as we do at Sgoil Eanna and get them to talk to the children'. Pearse considered the Montessori system the closest contemporary approximation to his ideals and his proposals for educational reform were coolly practical. He would raise teachers' salaries – male teachers earned on average less than policemen and engine drivers – 'for between the salaries offered to teachers and the excellence of a country's educational system there is a vital connection'. He would increase the authority of schools *vis à vis* the department of education, urging 'freedom to the individual school, freedom to the individual teacher, freedom as far as may be to the individual pupil'. But so far was he from neglecting administrative reality that he rightly recommended a more integrated department of education in place of the ludicrous sprawl of existing authorities, even while within the system 'teachers and not clerks would henceforth conduct the education of the country'. Far from considering ancient Irish customs the final court of appeal, he visualised his streamlined central authority serving as an active research centre on recent developments 'to keep the teachers in touch with educational thought in other lands', which the existing 'modern' authorities so conspicuously failed to do. And he insisted on investing his ancient Irish ideal with equality of educational opportunity: 'and this, remember, was not the education system of an aristocracy, but the education system of a people. It was more democratic than any education system in the world today'.

Pearse's theory of education cannot be said to have failed in Ireland. It has never been tried, not because a sensible people have rejected a misty archaic idea, but because their minds have lagged far behind such an uncompromisingly modernising concept of education, relentlessly subordinating birth to merit and the production of stereotyped anonymity to the fostering of individual personality.

Because it gave control over the crucial field of education Pearse supported the Council's bill, a form of local government which even a home rule convention spurned in 1907. Pearse likewise accepted the anaemic third Home Rule Bill in 1912, though warning that if it were rejected this time only rebellion remained as a final alternative. The Home Rule Bill passed the Commons a second time in July 1913, to be defeated once more in the Lords. In September the Ulster Unionist Council established a provisional government of Ulster, and the acquisition of guns by the Ulster Volunteers became public knowledge. Pearse, hitherto committed to home rule, now grasped that the initiative lay with Carson and Bonar Law, whose cool contempt for parliamentary majorities and the rule of law finally compelled all other parties involved in Irish politics to define their attitude towards violence.

Pearse had no doubt that force must be met by force: 'if you cannot arm otherwise than by joining Carson's volunteers, join Carson's volunteers. But you can, for instance, start volunteers of your own'. The Irish Volunteers were established in November 1913, under the leadership of Eoin MacNeill, professor of early Irish history in University College, Dublin, whose article, 'The North Began', published on 1 November, appealing for a volunteer force on the Ulster model, roused considerable public response. The home rule organs dismisssed the Irish Volunteers as either unnecessary, derisory or dangerous, and provoked Pearse to the most sanguinary writing of his life:

> I am glad, then, that the North has begun. I am glad that the Orangemen have armed for it is a goodly thing to see arms in Irish hands. I would like to see the A.O.H. armed. I would like to see the Transport Workers armed. I would like to see any and every body of Irish citizens armed. We must accustom ourselves to the

thought of arms, to the sight of arms, to the use of arms. We may make mistakes in the beginning and shoot the wrong people; but bloodshed is a cleansing and a sanctifying thing and a nation which regards it as the final horror has lost its manhood. There are many things more horrible than bloodshed; and slavery is one of them'.

When he concedes that 'we may . . . shoot the wrong people', Pearse recognised reality, refusing to seek refuge in Bonar Law's euphemistic 'there are things stronger than parliamentary majorities', and applying the 'we' to anyone willing to arm in defence of what they considered their rights, including Orangemen: 'The Orangeman is ridiculous in so far as he believes incredible things: he is estimable in so far as he is willing and able to fight in defence of what he believes. It is foolish of the Orangeman to believe that his personal liberty is threatened by home rule: but, in that he believes that, it is not only in the highest degree common sense but it is his clear duty to arm in defence of his threatened liberty'. As if anticipating critics who charged that he invoked bloodshed as an ideal, Pearse insisted that the appeal to force, however sincere the motivation, remained justifiable only as a last resort: 'obviously', he wrote in February 1916 'if any nation can obtain its freedom without bloodshed it is its duty so to obtain it . . . if England after due pressure were to say to us, here, take Ireland, no one would be so foolish as to answer, no, we'd rather fight you for it. But things like that do not happen. One must fight or at least be ready to fight'. Pearse's elaboration of the moral right of rebellion can only be understood as a response to the Orange appeal to violence and the home rule insistence that nationalists should refuse to take any similar steps and rely instead on the Liberal Government's assurances that it would not tolerate unionist defiance of parliament: 'the Orangeman who can fire a gun will certainly count for more in the end than the Nationalist who can do nothing cleverer than make a pun. The superseded Italian rifles which the Orangemen have imported may not be very dangerous weapons; but at least they are more dangerous than epigrams. When the Orangemen 'line the last ditch' they may make a very sorry show; but we shall make an even sorrier show, for we shall have to get Gordon Highlanders to line the ditch for us'.

Pearse abhorred the racist mentality of some Irish-Irelanders: 'I propose that we take *service* as our touchstone, and reject all other touchstones: and that, without bothering our heads about sorting out, segregating and labelling Irishmen and Irish women according to their opinions, we agree to accept as fellow nationalists all who specifically or virtually recognise this Irish nation as an entity and, being part of it, owe it and give it their service'. This definition creates its own problems. Who, for instance, defines 'virtually'? However, Pearse's desire to achieve a generous definition emerges clearly, as it does later when he reproves narrow linguistic nationalists: 'I challenge again the Irish psychology of the man who sets up the Gael and the Palesman as opposing forces with conflicting outlooks . . . he who would segregate Irish history and Irish men into two sections – Irish speaking and English speaking – is not helping toward achieving Ireland a Nation'. And, even as his thought became increasingly politicised he struggled towards an ever broader concept of nationalism. Whereas in 1907 he disapproved of Synge's *Playboy* almost as intently as he despised the mob who howled it down, by 1913 he reproached his earlier self: 'when a man like Synge, a man in whose sad heart there glowed a true love of Ireland, one of the two or three men who have in our time made Ireland considerable in the eyes of the world, uses strange symbols which we do not understand, we cry out that he has blasphemed and we proceed to crucify him'.

Pearse repudiated not merely the totalitarian, but the orthodox conservative authoritarian concept of the state. To the pragmatic Pearse the State was always a means, never an end in itself. However emphatically he asserted that 'there have been states in which the rich did not grind the poor, although there are no such states now; there have been free self-governing democracies, although there are few such democracies now; there have been rich and beautiful social organisations, with an art, a culture and a religion in everyman's house, though for such a thing today we have to search out some sequestered people living by a desolate seashore or in a high forgotten valley among lonely hills . . .,' he sought salvation not by retreating to these fringes, but by bringing art, culture and religion into the factories and cities. 'A free Ireland would not, and could not, have hunger in her fertile vales and squalor in her cities. Ireland has resources to feed five times her population; a free Ireland will make those resources available. A free Ireland would drain the bogs, would harness the rivers, would plant the wastes, would nationalise the railways and the waterways, would improve agriculture, would protect fisheries, would foster industries, would promote commerce, would diminish extravagant expenditure (as on needless judges and policemen), would beautify the cities, would educate the workers, (and also the non-workers, who stand in dire need of it), would, in short, govern herself as no external power – nay, not even a government of angels and archangels – could govern her'. However imaginative this programme, it can hardly be considered an arcadian hymn against either industrialisation or the economic role of the state. Pearse would increase the state's role in economic life, because private enterprise had patently failed to display enterprise, but he would simultaneously limit its control of education, because 'man is not primarily a member of a state, but a human individuality'. It is to the primacy of the individual personality that Pearse constantly returns, whether in his educational theories, or in his political tracts: 'the end of freedom is human happiness; the end of national freedom is individual freedom: therefore individual happiness'. He insisted on universal adult suffrage and supported the suffragettes: 'to restrict the franchise in any respect is to prepare the way for some future usurpation of the rights of the sovereign people. The people, that is, the whole people, must remain sovereign not only in theory, but in fact'.

Pearse, frequently more passionate than profound, failed to create a synthesis between his conflicting ideals – Christ and Cuchulainn, compassion and strength, 'I would be gentle but not soft'; national solidarity and individual freedom, 'the right to national freedom is made to rest on its true basis, the right to individual freedom'; the Hero and the sovereignty of the people, 'perhaps the people itself will be its own Messiah'; instinct and intellect – having asserted that 'I doubt if a theory of nationality be a very great gain, and plainly the instinct of a Fenian artisan was a finer thing than the soundest theory of the Gaelic League professor', he devoted his final four tracts to developing a theory of nationality! But he was an honest thinker, and his non-sequitors spring from logical confusion, not from ideological expediency. Shades of Sorel, Maurras and Corradini loom from Pearse's pages, but superficial similarities with contemporary continental neo-romantics or proto-fascists conceal fundamental differences. Part of Pearse's fascination in the broader context, indeed, lies in his demonstration that the assumptions he shared with many of these thinkers could lead to an affirmation of modernising rather than reactionary principles.

Pearse's later thought owes something to the influence of James Connolly. Connolly founded the Irish Socialist Republican Party on his arrival in Dublin from Edinburgh in 1896. The timing appeared propitious, for the urban working classes were becoming increasingly restive. The Belfast Labour party, a branch of the (English) Independent Labour Party, was established in 1892. The Irish Trades Congress, founded in 1894, recruited about 70,000 members, mostly skilled workers organised in craft unions, by 1910. But Connolly, too abrasive and theoretical, failed to make much progress, and left for America in 1903. It was Jim Larkin, an emigrant's son who arrived in Belfast from Liverpool in 1907 to organise primarily unskilled labour in the docks, who dominated the labour scene from then until 1913. After a hectic career in Belfast, where his initial successes failed to more than momentarily bridge the sectarian gap among workers, Larkin came to Dublin in 1908, where, breaking away from the (English) National Dockers' Union, he established the Irish Transport and General Workers' Union. Membership of the ITGWU rose to 10,000 by 1913, when Larkin challenged William Martin Murphy, the most influential businessman in Dublin, by attempting to organise the workers of Murphy's United Tramways' Company in his union. When Murphy refused to recognise the union, Larkin called a strike on 26 August, which soon spread to several connected trades as the employers locked out all members of Larkin's union. Passions ran high, particularly when police arrested Larkin, killed two labour demonstrators and wounded 400 in O'Connell Street in September. British supporters sent £150,000 assistance, but when Larkin foolishly denounced the Trades Union Congress, his main source of financial support, for refusing to encourage sympathetic strike action in England, the flow of funds sharply declined. The employers, confident of starving the men and especially their women and children, into submission, refused to accept arbitration, and by January 1914 had effectively won, as more and more men slunk back to work on condition that they did not join the union. But though the employers won the battle, they lost the war. Larkin had broken the bond of deference and had created a conscious sense of identity among the unskilled workers, the most degraded single sector of Irish society. Never again did Dublin businessmen dare employ mass starvation as a weapon against their workers. The ITGWU was not destroyed, as the employers hoped, but Larkin left for America in October 1914. James Connolly, who returned from America to become an ITGWU organiser in Belfast in 1911, now emerged as the dominant figure among Dublin unskilled workers, both through his role in the union and his activity in the Citizen Army, which was founded on 23 November 1913 from a small body of workers who were inspired by the example of the Ulster Volunteers to put their unoccupied time during the lockout to constructive use. When the workers of the world flocked to kill each other at the bidding of their nationalist masters in the first world war, Connolly was cured of his illusion that socialist solidarity could prevent international conflict. He decided, in effect, that the road to socialism lay through nationalism, and determined to commit the Citizen Army to insurrection. He was dissuaded from going it alone with his few hundred Citizen Army men in January 1916 only by an IRB promise to rise at Easter.

James Connolly was a cantankerous man. He had a genius, even in the faction ridden company he kept, for quarrelsomeness. He was also, by some considerable distance, the most remarkable man of his generation in Irish politics. Born in Edinburgh in 1868, the son of emigrants, he suffered hardships that would have left most of his contemporaries in public life broken wrecks. He learned to read by the light of the fire, scratching out the alphabet with the charred embers. He started work at the age of eleven, drifting from one dead-end job to another until finally graduating to his father's occupation of manure carter. Yet, for sheer originality, his writings on modern Irish history, flung down at odd moments snatched from the daily grind of eking out a miserable living, are, despite their many flaws, worth those of all his professional contemporaries combined. He was the only unskilled labourer among European socialist intellectuals, and one of the few intellectuals among European trade unionists.

What Connolly lacked, and it was a fatal deficiency from the viewpoint of achieving a socialist Ireland, was an adequate theory of political power. Confronted in a particularly acute form with the three evil geniuses of socialism – priest, patriot and peasant – Connolly had little idea how to handle them. He made a major theoretical contribution to reconciling Catholicism and socialism, but failed to get the message across to most Catholics. Orange and A.O.H. bigotry in Belfast frustrated his endeavours to bridge sectarian hatred among workers in 1911–12. In Dublin Pearse was with him in spirit, if not always in theory, but few other republicans displayed much interest in socialism. His fatal tactical error was his reluctance to acknowledge the existence of rural Ireland. His Edinburgh life had made him a 'townie' to the core. The programme of his socialist party in 1896 contains almost nothing on agriculture. His solitary excursion to south-west Ireland brought clear insight into the economic problems of small farms, but no understanding of peasant psychology. Connolly's experience outside Ireland was limited to British and American labour circles, among the few socialist movements not faced by a major 'peasant question'. He thus remained largely oblivious to the feverish questioning by Jaures, Bernstein and Lenin of the orthodox Marxist position concerning the passive role of the peasantry in a socialist revolution.

In one respect it was shrewd tactics to ally with the republicans, the only nationalists who might conceivably pry Ireland loose from the grip of the obesely bourgeois home rule party. But by allowing himself to become involved in the blood sacrifice of Easter week Connolly buried Irish socialism for several decades. Blood sacrifice made some sense in Pearse's eschatology, but none at all in Connolly's. Nationalists are as useful to their cause dead as alive, but there was only one Connolly. The prospects for socialism were slender in any event, but Connolly's death ensured that whatever phoenix rose from the embers of Easter would unfurl no red flag.

It is true that, although Connolly realised he was going to his death when he led 200 men of the Citizen Army out on Easter Monday morning, he had not planned it that way. Nor, indeed, had the republicans. They, like Connolly, accepted the possibility of a blood sacrifice, but only as a contingency plan, not as the main objective of all the preparations of the five preceding years.

The Rising of 1916

Tom Clarke returned in 1907 from America, where he had gone in 1898 after serving 15 years penal servitude for his part in a Fenian dynamiting campaign. The struggle waged by himself, Sean MacDermott and Bulmer Hobson to revitalise the IRB culminated in a victory over the old somnolent IRB leaders in 1911, when Clarke became treasurer and MacDermott secretary of the Supreme Council. But Clarke and MacDermott, who became the key organiser, had no notion of a blood sacrifice at that stage. IRB representatives secured influential positions in the Irish Volunteers in November 1913, but when membership rose to 27,000 by May 1914

John Redmond decided to bring the volunteers under his own control by packing the provisional committee with his nominees in June. On 26 July over 1,000 guns were landed at Howth, in pale imitation of the Larne gun-running, and later that day the Scottish Borderers won a famous victory in Bachelor's Walk, killing three people and wounding 38 by firing on a crowd taunting them with their hamhanded failure to capture the rifles. Recruitment to the volunteers immediately soared and membership reached 179,000 by September.

The first world war shattered the volunteers, for only about 10,000 of them remained with the anti-war, primarily republican Irish Volunteers when Redmond founded the National Volunteers to support the English war effort. Redmond, like many others, believed the war would be short. Had Southern Ireland, in contrast to the Ulster volunteers, not participated in the war, British public opinion would certainly have decisively rejected any attempt to coerce Ulster unionists. Partition would have been inevitable. A knowledge of Ulster history would have made it plain that partition was inevitable in any event, but because Redmond chose to consider Orange convictions the artificial product of continuing English conspiracy instead of inherent in Orange consciousness, his strategy still depended on the liberal alliance, and thus on English public opinion. The Home Rule Bill actually became law in September 1914, but its implementation was suspended for the duration of the war. Redmond might conceivably have secured home rule for Southern Ireland there and then by refusing support for the war except on condition of immediate self-government, but he certainly could not have won east Ulster. The irony was that the liberal alliance, the lynchpin of home rule strategy since 1886 came to a *de facto* end when Carson and Bonar Law were included in a coalition war ministry in May 1915.

The IRB welcomed the war, but not because it proffered opportunities for a blood-sacrifice. On the contrary, the IRB clung to the hallowed principle, 'England's danger, Ireland's opportunity'. Negotiations for German aid, and the decision to restrain Connolly from a premature insurrection in January 1916, were not based on blood sacrifice theory, but on careful calculation of the odds. Discouraging though these odds might be, they were not hopeless. There were only about 6,000 troops and 10,000 armed policemen in the country, compared with a potential maximum of about 18,000 volunteers. Had a substantial proportion of these turned out and had they been armed with the 20,000 rifles and ammunition which the German ship, the *Aud,* was due to land in Kerry just before Easter, a protracted struggle might have ensued, with the possibility of increasing public support as fighting progressed. However problematical the odds, they were incomparably the best likely to occur for a very long time by IRB criteria. No wonder that the leaders rejected Eoin MacNeill's tortuous argument that a rising would be morally unjustified without reasonable hope of success, but that resistance to being disarmed would be morally justified. If MacNeill deemed the objective circumstances of 1916 hopeless he was in effect saying that a rising would never be justified, so what was the point of acquiring arms in the first instance? And as the government would presumably choose to disarm the volunteers when it considered the circumstances most propitious, the prospects of resistance would presumably be even less promising than a surprise volunteer initiative.

Only when the plans for landing the German arms miscarried on Holy Thursday–Good Friday, 1916, and MacNeill, discovering he had been deceived by IRB leaders about the projected rising, cancelled the manoeuvres – in effect, the rising – scheduled for Easter Sunday, 23 April, did the issue of a blood sacrifice arise.

The leaders accepted the challenge, but they did not welcome it. Even Pearse, who consciously cultivated the concept of blood sacrifice as a last resort, was extremely depressed after MacNeill's countermanding order. Pearse did not, after all, fulfil his own prophecy, 'I will take no pike, I will go into battle with bare hands', Until MacNeill's countermanding order on Easter Sunday, he had hoped to win. The final decision to rise on Easter Monday, taken by the military council on Sunday, was partly a defensive one, prompted by the belief that Dublin Castle was about to arrest the leaders as it had swooped on the Fenians in 1865.

However romantic its overtones, the proclamation of the republic, which Pearse read to a sceptical audience outside the general post office, the rebel headquarters, on Easter Monday, was dedicated to the modernisation of Irish society. It promised equality of political, social, economic and religious opportunity; 'The Republic guarantees religious and civil liberty, equal rights and equal opportunities to all its citizens, and declares its resolve to pursue the happiness and prosperity of the whole nation and of all its parts, cherishing all the children of the nation equally . . .'

The rebels were crushed within a week. Their tactics were amateurish, but their performance recorded a distinct improvement on the fiascos of 1803, 1848 and 1867. More soldiers than volunteers were killed, and the Widow McCormack's cabbage patch was buried forever beneath Mount Street bridge, where 13 volunteers took 231 Sherwood Foresters with them to their eternal reward. The ultimate psychological success of the rising owed almost everything to Pearse's humanitarianism. The public response had been, at best, bafflement, at worst, hostility. Many of the poorer Dublin families, who had relatives serving in the British army, considered the rising a German plot. It was the executions, not the rising, that worked a sea change in public opinion. And there would hardly have been executions, except for Casement, but for the surrender, as the volunteer leaders would probably have died in action. Thomas MacDonagh obeyed Pearse's surrender order with great reluctance; Tom Clarke thought of suicide; Eamonn Ceannt never recognised the potential propaganda value of the executions, and denounced the futility of surrender in his final letter the night before his execution. The surrender was caused by the deaths of three civilians, caught in army fire under Pearse's gaze. These civilian fatalities so shocked Pearse that he immediately decided to surrender to avoid further civilian casualties, instead of attempting to beat a fighting retreat, as he originally planned.

The British commander, General Maxwell, who had spent much of his life teaching lessons to natives in Egypt, determined to teach the same lesson to natives nearer home. Maxwell was not a particularly inhumane man, but he behaved as the *agent provocateur* of a nation. There were only two sensible alternatives open to him – either a massive dose of terror, including large scale execution of prisoners, to cower all potential resistance, or else the ridicule of immediate release. Maxwell chose precisely the course calculated to rouse maximum resentment and minimum fear. His execution of 15 leaders was to prove one of England's less remunerative educational investments.

Sinn Féin

Sinn Féin (ourselves), established by Arthur Griffith in 1905, was not directly involved in the rising. Griffith believed that English military power made rebellion impractical, and advocated instead a Dual Monarchy, vaguely modelled on the precedents of Grattan's Parliament and the Austro-Hungarian arrangement of 1867. He felt this could be achieved through passive resistance.

Irish members should abstain from Westminster, and help establish an alternative administration in Ireland by assisting in gradually implementing a 15 point policy to achieve industrialisation through state capitalism. This policy appeared chimerical to the ordinary voter, as indeed it was, for most of the objectives could not be achieved if Britain chose to oppose them. Passive resistance could be successful only if supported by active resistance. Sinn Féin won only one-quarter of the votes in the North Leitrim by-election in 1908, many of them probably personal votes for its candidate C. J. Dolan, the sitting member, who had resigned from the Home Rule party. It contested no further parliamentary elections until 1917, and exerted little influence on events before 1916. The government had such little grasp of affairs, however, that it promptly labelled the rising a Sinn Féin rebellion, and Sinn Féin generally came to be used as an umbrella term for the anti-home rule nationalist movement in the following years.

But the new Sinn Féin bore only limited relationship to the old. It was taken over by republicans. In October 1917 Griffith stood down as president in favour of de Valera, the senior surviving leader of the rising, who swept to a crushing victory over the home rule candidate in the East Clare by-election in July 1917. The Clare result came as no great surprise, for the direction of the electoral tide had become clear in February 1917 when Count Plunkett comfortably won North Roscommon. The rising itself had been an essentially Dublin affair. Both Sinn Féin and the IRB were primarily urban, indeed almost metropolitan, movements. Roscommon therefore posed an intriguing challenge for Plunkett was selected as Sinn Féin candidate mainly because he was the father of an executed rebel leader, and made no pretence of campaigning on local issues. Roscommon was flourishing from the high war-time agricultural prices, and there seemed little objective reason why Sinn Féin should perform any better in February 1917 than it had in neighbouring Leitrim in February 1908. Yet Plunkett cantered home.

David Lloyd George, who succeeded Asquith as English prime minister in 1916, released all 1916 prisoners by June 1917 and convoked the Irish Convention in July to encourage representatives of all shades of Irish opinion reconcile their divergent views. The convention, predictably, failed to resolve anything. Sinn Féin refused to attend, and Ulster unionists revealed once more an eloquent command of the vocabulary of negation. Nevertheless the convention recorded the conversion of many Anglo-Irish, as distinct from the Scotch-Irish, to some form of home rule. It was to prove of the highest importance for the nature of the emerging state that a substantial section of the Anglo-Irish, even at the eleventh hour, should begin to adopt a positive attitude towards the implications of their vanished supremacy.

The general election of 1918

The swing to Sinn Féin recorded in four by-election victories in 1917 seemed to have been halted, when the Home Rule party retained three hard-fought seats in early 1918. The government's threat to impose conscription in April, and its arrest of most Sinn Féin leaders in May on the pretext of their involvement in a 'German plot' to promote revolt in Ireland, has frequently been considered decisive in retrieving Sinn Féin's flagging fortunes. In June, Arthur Griffith won the East Cavan by-election, and in the general election in December the party won 73 seats compared with the Unionists 26 and the Home Rulers 6.

The defeated parties vigorously disputed Sinn Féin's claim of overwhelming victory, pointing out that it won only forty-seven per cent of the votes cast compared with sixty-nine per cent of the seats. However, 25 Sinn Féin members were returned unopposed. The fact that home rule strength in the contested constituencies declined from east to west – home rulers won forty-nine per cent of the vote in Louth, forty-eight per cent in North Wexford, forty-two per cent in South Wexford, but their highest vote in Connacht was thirty-four per cent; and in Munster, outside Waterford city, only thirty per cent – supports the assumption that they withdrew in the constituencies where they were weakest. Had the 25 walkover seats been contested, the Sinn Féin proportion of the total vote would probably have risen from forty-seven per cent to about sixty per cent.

Hostile observers adduced three main reasons for Sinn Féin success – the conscription threat, the party's superior machine, and intimidation of home rule supporters. Changes in constituency boundaries complicate comparison with earlier by-election results, but even a crude analysis casts doubt on the assertion that the Sinn Féin failure to win South Armagh in February 1918, Waterford city in March and East Tyrone on 4 April indicated a rapid decline in popular support, reversed only by the threat of conscription announced on 9 April. The two corresponding Ulster constituencies were not contested in December. In the five seats contested by both Nationalist parties in the present six-county area, however, Sinn Féin won only forty-two per cent of the total anti-Unionist vote. This suggests that the thirty-seven per cent and forty per cent votes for Sinn Féin in the two spring by-elections reflected continuing vitality, not atrophy.

Captain Redmond, home rule winner in Waterford city in March, defeated the same opponent in December. As Redmond was the only home rule victor in southern Ireland, Waterford city must be considered the most unrepresentative single constituency in the country.

Few inferences can be drawn from the by-election results in early 1918 about a waning of Sinn Féin support immediately prior to the conscription threat.

It is true that the home rule machine had not been tested in some areas since 1885. But Sinn Féin's machine had never been tested nationally at all. The home rule machine performed efficiently in 1910 in 9 of the constituencies the party failed to contest in 1918. As late as November 1916 the nationalist machine functioned so smoothly in the West Cork by-election that Daniel O'Leary could predict his majority to within 11 votes in a poll of 3,500.[52] Yet, despite optimistic initial reports of the favourable response to the same O'Leary's 'exhaustive canvass of West Cork' in November 1918, he soon withdrew.[53] So did Captain Donellan in East Cork, conqueror of the redoubtable William O'Brien in a hard-fought seventy-six per cent poll in 1910, and W. G. Fallon, who candidly conceded after a preliminary canvass that he stood no chance in mid-Cork.[54] William Doris, who secured eighty per cent of the vote in North Mayo in 1910 could win only fourteen per cent in 1918. The home rule machine was caught no more unprepared in the Leitrim by-election of 1908 when it captured seventy-five per cent of the votes, than in 1918 when it won less than twenty per cent. Machinery, in short, reflected morale.

'Intimidation' customarily constitutes the most sophisticated level of comprehension to which the jilted suitor aspires in assuaging his wounded vanity. The evidence decisively refutes 'intimidation' as a serious explanation of Sinn Féin success. *The Freeman's Journal,* the main home rule newspaper, conceded that 'with a few exceptions polling passed off without untoward incidents'[55] and detailed local reports bore out the claim of the *Irish Independent* that, despite occasional local disorders during the campaign 'nobody who remembers the scenes of violence which took place at the general election which followed the Parnell split could fail to note with the liveliest satisfaction the contrast between then and now'.[56] Even in East Mayo, the worst constituency for intimidation during the campaign, where de Valera was pitted against John Dillon, the *Freeman* noted that the actual polling was 'fortunately not marked by the violence and intimidation which was anticipated'.[57] Although Dillon lost heavily, he probably retained a substantial personal following for he won thirty-four per cent of the vote compared with his party's twenty per cent in West Mayo and fourteen per cent in North Mayo, where 'the election was conducted in an entirely peaceful manner'. In Dublin city 'the polling was practically without incidents, the utmost good order and good humour prevailing throughout the day'; in Cork city the election was 'perhaps the quietest on record'; in South Kilkenny it was 'remarkable for the good humour which has prevailed from the date of nomination to the date of the poll'; in Louth 'the polling was without incident', and in Meath, bitter battlefield of 1892, 'the elections passed off without a solitary unpleasant incident'.[58] The worst intimidation recorded in Munster occurred in Waterford city, where home rule supporters harrowed Sinn Féin. The final word can be left with Sir Thomas Esmonde. Instead of attributing to intimidation his defeat in a close contest in North Wexford, he conceded, in words applicable to most constituencies, that 'it had been a thoroughly good humoured election, and nothing had happened that any of them would regret. The people had unquestionably declared their decision'.[59] Sinn Féin won, in short, because of overwhelming support for its policy within Southern Ireland.

But what was Sinn Féin policy? Nothing more clearly reflects the political sophistication of Sinn Féin than the adroitness with which it evaded this question. Its specific campaign commitments remained elusive and ambiguous.

Virtually the only Sinn Féin speaker to permit a definite promise sully his lips was Fr Michael O'Flanagan, who suggested that the party would raise old age pensions from 7/6 to 10/- a week. Sinn Féin did not proclaim a war-platform in the election, any more than in the earlier by-elections. De Valera himself had assured Clare voters that 'those who went out in Easter Week had achieved their ends, and another Easter Week would be a super-fluity'.[60] The country simply did not believe John Dillon, who took as his theme 'you cannot have an Irish Republic until you fight and defeat England'.[61] Sinn Féin limited itself to promising abstention from Westminster and attendance at the Versailles peace conference. It ignored the query, what if the peace conference refused to recog-nise them? It was because Sinn Féin did not advocate armed rebellion that Cardinal Logue felt justified in allocating it four of eight Ulster seats when he arbitrated between the two nationalist parties to avoid splitting the anti-unionist vote. The very fact that Sinn Féin agreed to accept the cardinal's arbitration pointed to its *trans-formismo* grasp of nationalist political reality, its willingness to act as a popular front of nationalist forces. Fancy the Fenians accepting arbitration by Cardinal Cullen! Fancy Cullen allocating disputed seats to a Fenian!

The election debate was really about deference. The electorate was invited to pronounce its verdict on the spirit of Easter week, to adjudicate on the tone of the debate with England. To the majority of voters home rule had always simply meant independence. As early as 1879 James Daly, the anti-Fenian land leaguer, defined his concept of home rule as 'a complete, an unqualified control of Irish affairs by the Irish people'. The main objection most home rule leaders had to physical force was simply that it was doomed to defeat. Their objection to the 'impossibilists' was a strictly practical, not a moral or aesthetic one. William O'Brien summed up the popular attitude: 'the methods vary with the circumstances . . . mere methods are accidents, not principles'. Public opinion was reconciled to the loss of several parliamentary battles. But it demanded that the Home Rule party never forget its commitment to ceaseless struggle. And it gradually lost this conviction under John Redmond's avuncular later leadership. For Redmond, more a Buttite than a Parnellite, increasingly saw his ideal role as essentially that of a dominion statesman rather than as leader of a small but fiercely independent people.

Epilogue

Pre-famine Ireland, though far from static, had been in many respects a tenaciously traditional society. The fatalistic response of so many famine victims eloquently expressed their primitive concept of the nature of society. Young Ireland might invoke damnation on a government which permitted starvation; John Mitchel's wrath at the righteous callousness of the official mind might mould the minds of generations – but of later generations, undergoing rapid politicisation in new societies, at home and abroad, who came to retrospectively denounce as a vicious conspiracy what the victims themselves no more attributed to human malevolence than victims of the famine of 1741 blamed the then government for their plight. The distinction popularly drawn a generation later, though rarely by contemporaries, that God sent the blight but the government created the famine, however historically oversimplified, marked a crucial advance in the modernisation of the Irish mind. Governments, unlike God, were amenable to pressures other than prayer. The implications of the growing conviction that the solution to famine lay within human control were drawn thirty years later by the Land League, which marked, in this rather significant respect, the definitive modernisation of the peasant mind.

In 1845 the Catholic Irish – for practical purposes the potential separatists – comprised nearly twenty-five per cent of the population of the United Kingdom, in 1918 only about seven per cent. Yet the dwindling proportion proved an increasingly sharp thorn in the British side, which suggests that its leaders were no mean players of the great game of politics. But the leaders could hardly have exerted such influence on even the peculiarly vulnerable British political system but for the solidarity and morale of their followers. Extensions of the franchise in 1850, 1868 and 1884, culminating in the near trebling of the electorate in 1918, from 0·7 to 1·9 million, when men aged between 21 and 30, and women over 30 got the vote, brought a considerable accretion of potential electoral strength to the nationalist cause. But sharp increases in the size of the electorate might mean little in prepolitical societies. Turnout in the first Italian general election under universal suffrage, in 1913, barely reached fifty per cent. The masses of north-western Europe did become gradually politicised in the course of the nineteenth century, but Ireland probably exhibited a higher level of political consciousness than any society at a comparable stage of economic development. Certainly, however retarded in other respects unionists found it psychologically imperative to consider the Irish, a lack of political consciousness rarely featured prominently on their indefatigable lists of inherent Irish vices. But politicisation by no means necessarily involved the assertion of national identity. Wales experienced a marked intensification of political consciousness between 1860 and 1880. But this simply resulted in a massive swing from Tory to Liberal in party allegiance. The general election of 1868 pointed to a similar possibility in Ireland. The analogy is not perfect, for the margin of the Liberal victory was deceptive. But a marriage of convenience might have ripened, in propitious circumstances, into a love match, and it is plausible enough to suggest that the result seemed to portend Ireland's imminent integration into the British Celtic fringes. That the Liberal triumph turned to ashes in the lifetime of a single parliament owed more to the amnesty movement for Fenian prisoners than to anything else. In this respect O'Donovan Rossa's victory in the Tipperary by-election of November 1869, though he himself was unseated and the verdict narrowly reversed three months later, marks the birth of modern Irish politics. O'Connell's triumph in Clare in 1829 had been primarily Catholic rather than national. Dramatic though the Sinn Féin victories of 1917–18 may have been, they were won against a Home Rule party with much the same ultimate political aspirations as itself. But Rossa defeated the Catholic candidate of a Unionist party that had swept to unprecedented electoral victory the previous year.

Thomas Davis wrote in 1845 that 'the fairies and the banshee, the poor scholar and the ribbonman, the Orange Lodge, the illicit still, and the faction fight are vanishing into history'. Much indeed was disappearing, and many concluded that malevolent English influence obliterated 'historic' Ireland. But modernisation involved the destruction of most of these features of traditional rural life in any event. They were disappearing all over western Europe as the parish ceased to form the mental boundary of the masses. In Ireland this natural obliteration process became confused to some extent with the attempt of the government to forge a new consciousness of their happy English heritage among the masses, primarily by pumping propaganda through the educational system. The native mind was indeed transformed, but not in the desired direction. Disraeli described the Irish question in 1844: 'A dense population inhabit an island where there is an established church which is not their church; and a territorial aristocracy, the richest of whom live in a distant capital'. By 1918 the population was no longer dense, the Church no longer established, the aristocracy neither here nor there. Yet the Irish question still refused to conform to unionist illusion. It was this capacity for sustaining, while simultaneously transforming, the question, more remarkable by far than simply dying in the last ditch, that testified to the real resilience of Irish identity.

Thomas Davis was, of course, guilty of false analogy and still falser prophecy, when he equated the Orange Lodge with the banshee, the illicit still, and even the ribbonman, as vanishing phenomena. For the other items on his list were characteristic of a specific stage of economic development. But Orangeism was racism, and thus essentially impervious to economic change. It retained a tenacious hold on Scotch-Irish loyalties throughout the whole period, fiercely resisting the contamination of equality of opportunity for Catholics. It remained to be seen in 1918 what policy Sinn Féin would adopt towards the Scotch-Irish. The nationalist attitude, republican and home rule alike, was a remarkable one. Almost alone among the peoples of Europe Irish nationalists aspired to integrate, rather than expel, the settler race. They offered the Scotch-Irish a more generous federal solution than any emerging European nationality offered its settlers, but stubbornly refused to recognise a Scotch-Irish right to self-determination. And while claiming the Scotch-Irish as Irish, they behaved as if all their traditions, and not merely Orangeism, were irreconcilably alien to everything Irish. The nationalist reluctance to salute the Shankill's sacrifice on the Somme in July 1916 reflected Southern Ireland's implicit belief, despite its denials, in the 'two nations' theory. The slaughter of the Somme, where the stupidity of the generals was surpassed only by the indomitable bravery of the officers and men of the 36th (Ulster) Division, bereaved thousands of Ulster homes. Nationalists frigidly ignored the tragedy. True, Thiepval was a futile sacrifice from an Irish viewpoint – but no more futile than, for instance, Fredericksburg, in which nationalists felt instinctive pride.

The nationalist reaction to the Somme reflected widespread southern indifference to even the finest traditions of the Scotch-Irish. More immediately relevant was the extraordinary insensitivity of home rulers and Sinn Féin alike in accepting Cardinal Logue as arbitrator in the disputed Ulster constituencies in the general election of 1918. This confirmed unionists' deepest suspicions that home rule meant Rome rule. And it cast considerable doubt on the nationalist commitment to the separation of Church and State, one of the specialisations of function characteristic of the modernisation process. However little actual weight the Cardinal carried – indeed precisely because of the little weight he carried – in both home rule and Sinn Féin deliberations, their agreement to his arbitration reflected a quite extraordinary obtuseness to the intensity of Scotch-Irish feelings in this regard, and provided yet another reminder of the self-righteous nationalist refusal to perceive the depth of the emotional gulf separating the two communities.

In other respects, too, the prospects for continuing modernisation were not entirely propitious. The demise of the home rule party was a necessary, but by no means sufficient, prerequisite for further modernisation. The party had long lost the modernising drive of the 1880s. As was virtually inevitable in a one-party society over a period of forty years, it had become a byword for the use of influence, pull, connections, manipulation, and that favouritism of every kind which Pearse so detested. Its opposition to the extension of the Schools Meals Service and the medical benefits of the Insurance Act to Ireland indicated that it had now become more of a hindrance than a help to the creation of greater equality of social opportunity. It had settled complacently into the rut of mediocrity, and attracted few gifted young men of its own early vintage. By 1918 the Home Rule leaders were long exhausted volcanoes, with no obvious successors within the party.

But if the Home Rule party was played out, it remained far from clear that Sinn Féin's heart was in the struggle for modernisation. The executions in 1916 removed the influence of the modernising intellectuals. Neither de Valera nor Griffith, the two dominant figures at this stage in the new Sinn Féin, had hitherto shown much interest in equality of individual opportunity. Only time would tell whether the general post office had been the cradle or the coffin of the revolution of the modernising intellectuals. It remained to be seen also whether it had been primarily force of character or force of circumstances that had generally associated nationalism with the struggle for political, religious and social equality of opportunity, and unionism with the rearguard action against modernisation.

The modernisation process suffered, of course, many set-backs between 1848 and 1918. Religious discrimination had, outside the north-east, declined markedly. The threat of eviction no longer exercised degrading sway over the countryside, but economic and educational discrimination remained rampant. The equality of opportunity proffered to agricultural labourers was little more than the opportunity to emigrate. A striking dichotomy persisted between the retarded rate of economic growth and the rapid rate of politicisation. Yet, Southern Ireland modernised probably as quickly as any other western European society during this period. At any rate few peoples had as striking a tale to tell as the story of the remarkable journey from the famine pits of 1848 to the Sinn Féin triumph of 1918.

Bibliographical Note

AFTER listing some general surveys, the bibliography, which is necessarily severely selective, is arranged according to chapter contents. Unless otherwise stated, the place of publication is London.

General Surveys: The final chapters of J. C. Beckett's excellent textbook *The Making of Modern Ireland 1603–1923* (1966) and the limpid essays by E. R. R. Green, T. W. Moody and D. MacCartney in T. W. Moody and F. X. Martin (ed.) *The Course of Irish History* (Cork 1966) provide succinct surveys. F. S. L. Lyons, *Ireland since the Famine* (1971) smoothes some sharp edges, but it may well be considered, in its astonishing range, enviable clarity and massive learning, the Oxford history of Ireland. Oliver McDonagh's masterly interpretive essay, *Ireland* (Englewood Cliffs 1968), a classic of controlled power and penetration, is the finest study of its type on the history of any European country known to me. Patrick O'Farrell, *Ireland's English Question* (1971) brilliantly sustains a beautifully honed but fundamentally untenable argument. N. Mansergh, *The Irish Question 1840–1921* (1965) remains the most sensitive study of the *Ideengeschichte* of any epoch of Irish history. L. J. McCaffrey, *The Irish Question 1800–1922* (Lexington 1968) provides a carefully structured account, while O. D. Edwards, 'Ireland' in O. D. Edwards, *et al. Celtic Nationalism* (1968) succeeds despite, or perhaps because of, a declamatory style, in evoking the atmosphere in which much nationalist thought was generated. E. Strauss, *Irish Nationalism and British Democracy* (1951) stimulatingly applies Marxist interpretive categories to rather refractory material. L. M. Cullen, *Life in Ireland* (1968) admirably pioneers the study of everyday life. Two exceptionally impressive German works, P. Alter, *Die irische Nationalbewegung zwischen Parlament und Revolution* (Munich 1971) and E. Rumpf, *Sozialismus und Nationalismus in Irland* (Meisenheim 1959) serve as timely reminders of the insularity of much of the English language historiography of Ireland. P. J. Corish (ed.), *A History of Irish Catholicism*, v, (Dublin, 1967–), and T. W. Moody and J. C. Beckett (ed.), *Ulster since 1800*, (two series, 1954, 1957) contain several valuable essays.

Chapter 1. Research on post-famine economic and social history has been severely handicapped by the lack of adequate compilations of statistics. The most useful existing collection, B. R. Mitchell and P. M. Deane, *Abstract of British Historical Statistics* (Cambridge 1962) should shortly be superseded by a volume published under the auspices of the *New History of Ireland*, which may be expected to give decided impetus to further work. K. H. Connell sketches a series of brilliant impressions of the rural social landscape in *Irish Peasant Society* (1968). Population changes are challengingly interpreted in A. Schrier, *Ireland and the American Emigration* (Minneapolis 1958); K. H. Connell 'Peasant Marriage in Ireland: its structure and Development since the Famine', in *Economic History Review*, xiv (1962) and 'Peasant Marriage in Ireland after the Great Famine', *Past and Present*, 12 (1957); S. H. Cousens, 'Emigration and Demographic Change in Ireland, 1851–61' *Economic History Review* 2nd series xiv (1961) and 'The Regional Variations in Population Changes in Ireland, 1861–1881' *ibid.* 2nd series xvii (1964); J. H. Johnston, 'Rural Population Changes in nineteenth century Londonderry', *Ulster Folk Life,* 15/16 (1970); B. M. Walsh, 'Marriage Rates and Population Pressure: Ireland 1871 and 1911' *Economic History Review* 2nd series xxiii (1970). Although primarily concerned with the contemporary scene, R. Crotty, *Irish Agricultural Production* (Cork 1966), one of the glories of twentieth-century Irish intellect, includes an exciting historical introduction, with some of whose conclusions I have, however, ventured to disagree in 'Irish Agriculture', *Agricultural History Review,* 17, (1969). P. M. A. Bourke has done more than anyone to raise the standards of the use of quantitative evidence in nineteenth-century history. His articles, 'The Agricultural Statistics of the 1841 Census of Ireland: A Critical Review', *Economic History Review* 2nd series xviii (1965) and 'Uncertainties in the Statistics of Farm Size in Ireland, 1841–1851', *Journal of the Statistical and Social Enquiry Society of Ireland* xx (1959–60) present fundamental revisions of long-accepted figures of farm sizes, livestock numbers and tillage acreages. P. Lynch and J. Vaizey, *Guinness's Brewery in the Irish economy, 1759–1875* (Cambridge 1960) contains a stimulating survey of post-famine development; for an exchange of views between the authors and myself, see 'Money and Beer in Ireland, 1790–1875' *Economic History Review,* 2nd series xix, (1966). James Meenan, *The Irish Economy since 1922,* (Liverpool 1970) is studded with useful data and sapient reflections on our period. J. C. Beckett and R. E. Glasscock (ed.) *Belfast: origin and growth of an industrial city* (1967), and L. M. Cullen (ed.) *The Formation of the Irish Economy* (Cork 1969) are useful collections of essays. E. Larkin's dazzling tour-de-force 'Economic growth, capital investment and the Roman Catholic church in nineteenth century Ireland', *American Historical Review,* lxxii (1967), is more convincing on the Catholic Church than on economic growth or capital investment. R. D. C. Black's deeply researched *Economic Thought and The Irish Question 1817–1870* (Cambridge 1960) makes an enduring contribution to the sadly neglected field of intellectual history. E. D. Steele, 'J. S. Mill and the Irish Question: the Principles of Political Economy, 1848–1865', and 'J. S. Mill and the Irish Question: Reform and the Integrity of the Empire, 1865–1870', *Historical Journal* xiii (1970) sensitively traces the development of Mill's thought. T. P. O'Neill *Fiontán Ó Leathlobhair* (Baile Átha Cliath 1962) scrupulously rescues Lalor from his disciples, while F. S. L. Lyons carefully reconstructs 'The economic ideas of Parnell' in M. Roberts (ed.) *Historical Studies,* II, (1959). R. B. McDowell, *The Irish Administration 1801–1914* (1964) summarises an extraordinary range of material. L. P. Curtis *Anglo-Saxons and Celts* (New York 1968) provides absorbing apercus about English attitudes. F. McGrath, *Newman's University, Idea and Reality* (1951), traces the fortunes of a fascinating experiment. T. W. Moody and J. C. Beckett, *Queen's University 1845–1949; The History of a University* vol. I, (1959) is a magisterial institutional study, and T. W. Moody, 'The Irish University Question in the Nineteenth Century', *History* xliii (1958) delicately unravels the tangled skein of the diplomacy of higher education. D. H. Akenson, *The Irish Education Experiment* (1969) provides an excellent survey of the administrative politics of primary education, while N. Atkinson, *Irish Education* (Dublin 1969) conveniently summarises scattered information on educational services at all levels. We lack sustained studies of the intellectual and social history of education, but M. MacCurtain (Sr Benvenuta) 'St. Mary's University College', *University Review,* iii, 4, and the short section devoted to nineteenth-century Ireland in H. F. Kearney, *Scholars and Gentlemen* (1971), afford tantalising glimpses of the possibilities inherent in this approach. Maureen

Wall clinically dissects 'The Decline of the Irish Language', in Brian Ó Cuiv (ed.) *The Fortunes of the Irish Language*, (Dublin 1969), which demolishes a host of comfortable popular illusions.

Chapter 2. J. H. Whyte conveniently summarises his authoritative book, *The Independent Irish Party 1850–59* (Oxford 1968) in a Dublin Historical Association pamphlet, *The Tenant League and Irish Politics in the Eighteen-Fifties* (Dundalk 1963). My interpretation of Paul Cullen relies heavily on the invaluable material collected in P. MacSuibhne, *Paul Cullen and his contemporaries, with their letters* (3 vols, Naas, 1961, 1962, 1965) and in E. R. Norman, *The Catholic Church and Ireland in the Age of Rebellion*, 1859–73 (1965), a splendid if rebarbative work, which the author has summarised and translated into English in a Dublin Historical Association pamphlet, *The Catholic Church and Ireland in the Eighteen-Sixties* (Dundalk 1965). K. T. Hoppen, 'Tories, Catholics and the General Election of 1859': *Historical Journal,* xiii (1970) illuminates many facets of higher electoral politics. T. W. Moody (ed.) *The Fenian Movement* (Cork 1968) is an indispensable introduction to Fenian studies, while Desmond Ryan, *The Fenian Chief* (Dublin 1967) and S. Ó Lúing, *Ó Donnabháin Rossa* (Iml. I, Baile Átha Cliath 1969) are revealing biographies of Fenian leaders. D. Thornley, *Isaac Butt and Home Rule* (1964), and L. J. McCaffrey, 'Irish Federalism in the 1870s: a study in conservative nationalism', *Transactions of the American Philosophical Society* (1962) contain penetrating analysis of the early home rule movement.

Chapter 3. T. W. Moody, 'The New Departure in Irish politics, 1878–79' in H. A. Cronne, T. W. Moody and D. B. Quinn (ed.) *Essays in honour of James Eadie Todd* (1949) remains the point of departure for all further work. T. N. Brown, *Irish-American Nationalism* (New York 1966) includes a probing analysis of American influences on the struggle for the land. C. C. O'Brien's brilliant *Parnell and his Party 1880–90* (Oxford 1957), J. L. Hammond's massive *Gladstone and the Irish nation* (1938), and W. O'Brien and D. Ryan (ed.) *Devoy's Post Bag* (2 vols. Dublin 1948, 1953) are essential.

Chapter 5. A number of admirable studies by F. S. L. Lyons analyse the personalities and policies of the Home Rule party: *Parnell* (Dublin Historical Association Pamphlet, Dundalk 1963), *John Dillon: A Biography* (1968), *The Fall of Parnell, 1890–91* (1960), *The Irish Parliamentary Party 1890–1910* (1951). C.C. O'Brien (ed.) *The Shaping of Modern Ireland* (1960) has a scintillating introduction and several perceptive essays. L. P. Curtis, Jr., *Coercion and Conciliation in Ireland, 1880–92; a study in Conservative Unionism* (Princeton 1963) and J. R. Fanning, 'The Unionist Party and Ireland, 1906–10', *Irish Historical Studies* xv (1966) explore the motives and techniques of Tory Policy. Systematic study of grassroots electoral history has hardly begun, but two perceptive general surveys by J. H. Whyte, 'The Influence of the Catholic Clergy on Elections in Nineteenth Century Ireland', *English Historical Review,* lxxv (1960) and 'Landlord influence at Elections in Ireland, 1760–1885' *ibid.* lxxx (1965), and M. Hurst's shrewdly argued 'The Secret Ballot Act and Ireland 1872', *Historical Journal,* 10 (1966) discuss central themes. H. J. Hanham, *Elections and Party management: Politics in the time of Disraeli and Gladstone* (1959) and J. R. Vincent, *The Formation of the Liberal Party, 1857–1868* (1966) contain interesting short sections on Ireland and are essential to an understanding of the general political system. A. T. Q. Stewart, *The Ulster Crisis* (1967) provides a clear, balanced account of Ulster Unionist attitudes: R. Blake, *Bonar Law: The Unknown*

Prime Minister (1955), and D. G. Boyce, British Conservative opinion, the Ulster question, and the partition of Ireland, 1912–21, *Irish Historical Studies,* xvii (1970) clarify the role of Ulster in Tory calculations; J. W. Boyle, 'The Belfast Protestant Association and the Independent Orange Order' *Irish Historical Studies,* xiii (1962) examines internal Orange power struggles.

Chapter 6. The history of labour movements is best approached through two fine biographies, E. Larkin, *James Larkin: Irish Labour Leader* (1965) and the more partisan C. Desmond Greaves, *The Life and Times of James Connolly* (1961), and a useful collection of Thomas Davis essays, J. W. Boyle (ed.) *Leaders and Workers* (Cork, n.d.). F. X. Martin (ed.) *Leaders and Men of the 1916 Rising* (1967) and K. B. Nowlan (ed.) *The making of 1916* (Dublin 1969) contain several thoughtful contributions. F. X. Martin, 'Eoin Macneill and the 1916 Rising', *Irish Historical Studies,* xii (1961), sheds fascinating light on the immediate background to the Rising. L. O Broin, *Dublin Castle and the 1916 Rising* (Dublin 1966) and *The Chief Secretary, Augustine Birrell and Ireland* (1969) skilfully reconstructs the workings of the official mind. M. Laffan, The Unification of Sinn Féin, 1917', *Irish Historical Studies,* xvii (1971), admirably fills a major gap, and Brian Farrell's luminous analysis, *The Founding of Dail Éireann* (Dublin 1971) broadens historiographical horizons by pioneering the disciplined application of comparative political theory to Irish experience.

References

[1]*Kilkenny Journal,* 17 Nov. 1849.

[2]*Northern Whig,* 16, 20 Apr. 1850.

[3]H. C. 1857–8 (2309) XXVI, *Report of the commissioners of Inquiry into the origin and character of the riots in Belfast in July and September 1857,* 250–4.

[4]*Ibid.,* 11.

[5]F. H. O'Donnell, *A History of the Irish Parliamentary Party* (1910), i, 371.

[6]M. Ryan, *Fenian Memories* (Dublin 1945), 44; *Ballinrobe Herald,* 16, 23 May, 6 June 1874.

[7]*Connaught Telegraph,* 2 Feb. 1878.

[8]*Special Commission Act, 1888. Reprint of the shorthand notes of the speeches, proceedings and evidence . . . taken before the Commissioners under the above-named Act,* 12 vols. (London 1890), vol. 10, q. 94, 598.

[9]*Tralee Chronicle,* 18 May 1880.

[10]*Connaught Telegraph,* 26 Apr. 1879.

[11]M. Davitt, *The Fall of Feudalism in Ireland* (1904), 146–7.

[12]*Connaught Telegraph,* 26 Apr. 1879.

[13]*Ibid.,* 14 June 1879.

[14]*Ibid.,* 17 July 1880; *Freeman's Journal,* 12 July 1880.

[15]*Report of Special Commission, 1888.* 1840 (c. 5891), XXVII, 566.

[16]*Ibid.,* 563–7.

[17]*Connaught Telegraph,* 24 June, 1 July 1882.

[18]*Ibid.,* 19 July 1879.

[19]These examples are taken from a valuable unpublished Nottingham Ph.D. thesis, C. J. Woods, *The Catholic Church and Irish politics* 1880–92 (1969).

[20]*Tralee Chronicle,* 1 Oct. 1880.

[21]*Freeman's Journal,* 17 Sept. 1881.

[22]*Report of Special Commission, 1888:* 1890 (c. 5891), XXVII, 567.

[23]*Annual Register,* 1880, 109.

[24]*Kilkenny Journal,* 24 Oct. 1849.

[25]*Tipperary Vindicator,* 20 Oct. 1849.

[26]Davitt, *op. cit.*, 164.

[27]*Special Commission Proceedings* 1890, vol. 10, q. 94, 630.

[28]*Connaught Telegraph*, 14 June 1879.

[29]*The Nation*, 2 Nov. 1878; *Connaught Telegraph*, 3 Apr. 1880, 31 Dec. 1881.

[30]H. C. 1881 (c–2779.I) XVIII, q. 17670.

[31]*Connaught Telegraph*, 14 June 1879, 8 May 1880.

[32]H. C. 1881 (c–2779.I) XVIII, q. 17268–9.

[33]Duke of Argyll, *The Irish Land Act, Nineteenth Century*, 1881.

[34]*Drogheda Argus*, 16 July 1892.

[35]*Westmeath Examiner*, quoted in *Roscommon Messenger*, 16 July 1892.

[36]*Drogheda Argus*, 23, 30 July 1892.

[37]*Tipperary Vindicator*, 30 Nov. 1869.

[38]*Ibid.*, 26 Nov. 1869.

[39]*Freeman's Journal*, 14 July 1892.

[40]M. Bodkin, *Recollections* (1914), 183.

[41]*Roscommon Herald*, 16 July 1892; Woods, *op. cit.*, 392.

[42]*Tuam Herald*, 16 July 1892.

[43]*Kilkenny Journal*, 24, 27, 31 Dec. 1890.

[44]*Tipperary Vindicator*, 30 Nov. 1869.

[45]*Ibid.*, 26 Nov. 1869; 8 Mar. 1870.

[46]*Connaught Telegraph*, 12 July 1879.

[47]*Ibid.*, 14 June 1879.

[48]*Tuam Herald*, 9 July 1892.

[49]*Clare Journal*, 18 July 1892.

[50]*Roscommon Herald*, 3, 10 Feb. 1917.

[51]*Freeman's Journal*, 29 Nov. 1918.

[52]*Cork Examiner*, 16, 17 Nov. 1916.

[53]*Freeman's Journal*, 26 Nov. 1918.

[54]*Cork Examiner*, 30 Nov. 1918.

[55]*Freeman's Journal*, 16 Dec. 1918.

[56]*Irish Independent*, 16 Dec. 1918.

[57]*Freeman's Journal*, 16 Dec. 1918.

[58]*Drogheda Independent*, 4 Jan. 1919.

[59]*Irish Independent*, 30 Dec. 1918.

[60]*Freeman's Journal*, 9 July 1917.

[61]*Ibid.*, 22 Nov. 1918.

Index